An Exploration in Mineral Supply Chain Mapping Using Tantalum as an Example

By Yadira Soto-Viruet, W. David Menzie, John F. Papp, and Thomas R. Yager

Open-File Report 2013–1239

U.S. Department of the Interior
U.S. Geological Survey

U.S. Department of the Interior
SALLY JEWELL, Secretary

U.S. Geological Survey
Suzette M. Kimball, Acting Director

U.S. Geological Survey, Reston, Virginia: 2013

For more information on the USGS—the Federal source for science about the Earth, its natural and living resources, natural hazards, and the environment—visit *http://www.usgs.gov* or call 1–888–ASK–USGS

For an overview of USGS information products, including maps, imagery, and publications, visit *http://www.usgs.gov/pubprod*

To order this and other USGS information products, visit *http://store.usgs.gov*

Suggested citation:
Soto-Viruet, Yadira, Menzie, W.D., Papp, J.F., and Yager, T.R., 2013, An exploration in mineral supply chain mapping using tantalum as an example: U.S. Geological Survey Open-File Report 2013–1239, 51 p., http://pubs.usgs.gov/of/2013/1239/.

Contents

Physical Properties of Tantalum 2
World Mine Production 2
Tantalum Refined Products and End Uses 3
Production of Mined Tantalum Minerals 3
Tantalum Processing Plants 5
Supply Chain for Tantalum 6
Tantalum Capacitors 7
Discussion and Conclusions 8
References Cited 9

Figures

1. Chart showing percentage of mined tantalum produced in the world in 2011, by country. 14
2. Chart showing refined tantalum (Ta) products, intermediate products manufactured from them,
    and the final goods produced 15
3. Significant tantalum (Ta) mines in the world. 16
4. Prospective tantalum (Ta) producers in the world 17
5. Significant tantalum (Ta) fabricators and refineries in the world. 18
6. Chart showing the relationship of selected tantalum (Ta) mines (or source materials) and processing
    facilities and their refined products 19
7. Chart showing tantalum (Ta) refineries in Japan and their products. 28
8. Chart showing selected tantalum capacitor manufacturers 29

Tables

1. Significant tantalum mines. 30
2. Prospective tantalum deposits and producers in the world. 36
3. Significant tantalum plants. 39
4. Locations of tantalum capacitor manufacturing facilities for three leading manufacturers. 42
5. Product name, description, and applications for selected tantalum capacitors produced by AVX Corp 43
6. Product name, product description, and applications for selected tantalum (Ta) capacitors produced by
    KEMET Corp. 44

Conversion Factors

SI to Inch/Pound

Multiply	By	To obtain
	Length	
kilometer (km)	0.6214	mile (mi)
meter (m)	1.094	yard (yd)
	Area	
square kilometer (km^2)	247.1	acre
square kilometer (km^2)	0.3861	square mile (mi^2)
	Mass	
megagram (Mg); metric ton (t)	1.102	ton, short (2,000 lb)
metric ton per year	1.102	ton per year (t/yr)
gram per metric ton (g/t)	0.03215	troy ounce per short ton

Temperature in degrees Celsius (°C) may be converted to degrees Fahrenheit (°F) as follows:
$°F=(1.8×°C)+32$

An Exploration in Mineral Supply Chain Mapping Using Tantalum as an Example

By Yadira Soto-Viruet, W. David Menzie, John F. Papp, and Thomas R. Yager

This report uses the supply chain of tantalum (Ta) to investigate the complexity of mineral and metal supply chains in general and show how they can be mapped. A supply chain is made up of all the manufacturers, suppliers, information networks, and so forth, that provide the materials and parts that go into making up a final product. The mineral portion of the supply chain begins with mineral material in the ground (the ore deposit); extends through a series of processes that include mining, beneficiation, processing (smelting and refining), semimanufacture, and manufacture; and continues through transformation of the mineral ore into concentrates, refined mineral commodities, intermediate forms (such as metals and alloys), component parts, and, finally, complex products. This study analyses the supply chain of tantalum beginning with minerals in the ground to many of the final goods that contain tantalum.

One of the great difficulties to overcome in mapping a supply chain is lack of transparency in the chain—whether it is related to the locations and types of facilities, the materials that the facilities consume and (or) produce, the facilities' production capacities, or the users of the products produced. Not knowing this information presents a significant barrier to understanding the risk of disruption in supply. Also, the geographic distribution of facilities may increase the risk of supply disruption if those facilities are dependent on the same infrastructure.

Supply chain mapping and analysis are tools used to identify the risks of disruption in supply. Each of the facilities that provide key components, perform particular processes, or produce goods is a node on a supply chain map; linkages between nodes are material flow paths. The supply chain nodes and paths constitute the supply chain structure. Singular nodes in a supply chain are unique facilities that provide a key component or perform a key process in the production of a good; they are sometimes called "pinch points."

Disruptions in a supply chain can occur when there is a significant change in the supply structure; the likelihood and possible magnitude of a disruption are determined in part by the characteristics of the chain. A supply chain with multiple facilities that perform each production process or that possess unused capacity (redundancy) is likely to be less subject to disruption—and to be more resilient—than a chain in which only one facility is able to perform a part of the production process or when the facilities in the chain are all operating at full capacity. Although there are significant benefits to redundancy in a supply chain, the cost of building and maintaining redundancy may be large enough to lead organizations to forego those benefits. Failures of production at singular nodes are more likely to cause disruptions in the production of a final good than are failures at redundant nodes. Singular nodes in the supply chain of a good may be difficult to identify, and failures of singular nodes can have surprising results. Multiple linkages suggest redundant material supply routes, implying a more robust supply chain.

A recent example of supply chain disruptions involving the failure of a singular node was owing to a natural disaster—the magnitude 9.0 earthquake and associated tsunami that struck Northern Honshu, Japan, on March 11, 2011. The earthquate and tsunami caused widespread devastation across the region, as tens of thousands of people were killed, hundreds of thousands of homes were damaged and (or) destroyed, and the commercial operations of firms were interrupted. The earthquake also disrupted a number of supply chains, so study of the event can provide some perspectives on supply chain disruption.

Northern Honshu is home to a large number of significant mineral production facilities, including nine cement plants, eight iodine plants, four iron and steel plants, four limestone mines, three copper facilities, two gold refineries, two lead refineries, two zinc refineries, one titanium dioxide plant, and one titanium dioxide sponge plant. Damage from the event resulted in a significant reduction in Japan's mineral production. Production of high-purity aluminum, cadmium, smelted and refined copper, and nickel in ferronickel was reduced by more than 10 percent, while production of ferroalloys, gold, lead, steel, silver, and zinc decreased by lesser amounts (Menzie and others, 2011; Kuo, 2013).

Much of the reduction in production was owing to the reduced availability of electricity and damage to important infrastructure, such as roads and ports, which affected the operations of many facilities. In some cases, damage to facilities affected only a particular site. In one case, damages to a singular node had surprising results. Titanium dioxide is used to make paint, and, because of the widespread use of paints, there are many such plants. Therefore, one would not have expected far-reaching consequences to result from damage to a single titanium dioxide plant. The plant in Northern Honshu, however, was the sole supplier of black and red paints used by Ford Motor Co. (United States) for a large number of its vehicles. The damage to the titanium dioxide plant interrupted the production of red and black vehicles of certain models until substitute paints could be identified. In this instance, the titanium dioxide plant constituted a singular node in the production chain (Naughton, 2011; Kuo, 2013).

Physical Properties of Tantalum

Tantalum is a transition metal with physical and chemical properties that are very similar to those of niobium. A refractory metal, tantalum is ductile, easily fabricated, resistant to corrosion by acids, and a good conductor of heat and electricity. Tantalum is also characterized by high melting and boiling points of 2,996 degrees Celsius (°C) and 5,425°C, respectively. The abundance of tantalum in the Earth's crust is 0.7 parts per million. Tantalum does not occur naturally as a free metal; however, tantalum occurs in a range of oxide mineral species, including ixiolite, microlite, tantalite, tapiolite, and wodginite. Tantalum-bearing mineral deposits are found in igneous rocks, which include carbonatites, granites, pegmatites, and syenites (British Geological Survey, 2011; Papp, 2012a; Roskill Information Services Ltd., 2012).

World Mine Production

In 2011, world mine production of tantalum increased by 7 percent to 706 metric tons (t) from 660 t in 2010. Rwanda accounted for 27 percent of total mine production in 2011; Brazil accounted for 20 percent; the Democratic Republic of the Congo [Congo (Kinshasa)], 15 percent; Ethiopia, 14 percent; China, 11 percent; Mozambique, 6 percent; Nigeria, 5 percent; and Burundi, 2 percent (fig. 1; Mobbs, 2012; Papp, 2013; Tse, 2013; Yager, 2013a–c).

The leading producers of tantalum have varied considerably since 2000. Australia, which was the leading producer from 2001 through 2008, ceased production in 2010, although it continues to have large resources of tantalum. For most years between 2001 and 2013, Brazil was the second ranked producer of tantalum. Since 2007, the proportion of production coming from Central Africa has increased. In 2011, production from Central Africa accounted for more than 40 percent of world production (Papp, 2009, 2010, 2011, 2012b).

Tantalum Refined Products and End Uses

Products made of refined tantalum include carbides, ingots, oxides, powders, and metal products, including plates, sheets, rods, and wires. Major industries that consume tantalum include the automotive, ceramic and surface coating, chemicals, construction, engineering, electronics, medical, and metallurgical industries, as well as the military. The electronics and metallurgical industries are the leading users of tantalum. The electronics industry accounts for about 50 to 60 percent of tantalum consumption, and the metallurgical industry accounts for about 20 percent of consumption. In the electronics industry, capacitors, which are the largest single end use for tantalum, accounted for about 40 percent of total tantalum consumption in 2011. Tantalum capacitors are intermediate manufactured products that are used in a variety of final goods, such as automotive electronics, cell phones, hard disc drives, light-emitting diodes, and personal computers. In the metallurgical industry, tantalum superalloys are used mainly in aerospace applications (such as jet engine blades) and land-based gas turbines. These superalloys contain from about 3 to 11 percent tantalum. Metallurgical products include sheets, plates, welded tubes, rods, and wires. These products account for about 8 to 11 percent of tantalum consumption (Roskill Information Services Ltd., 2012). Figure 2 shows the relationship among refined tantalum products, intermediate manufactured products, and final (consumer) goods.

Production of Mined Tantalum Minerals

Brazil and Rwanda, which were the leading producers of tantalum ore and concentrates in 2011, together accounted for 47 percent of the world's mine production of tantalum. The locations of significant tantalum mines and prospective producers are shown in figures 3 and 4, respectively, and selected deposits and producing areas are briefly discussed below. The mines and prospective producers are identified in tables 1 and 2, respectively, along with their annual capacities, facility type, ownership, and status. The numbers used to identify locations in figures 3 and 4 are keyed to the "ID" in tables 1 and 2, respectively.

Tantalum production in Australia stopped in 2010; however, Australia contains large resources of tantalum in the Greenbushes and the Wodgina deposits, and production is expected to resume in the future. Greenbushes is located about 250 kilometers (km) from Perth in southwestern Western Australia. The Greenbushes Mine, which is hosted by the Archean Greenbushes pegmatite and includes surface and underground workings, had a production capacity of about 550 metric tons per year (t/yr) of tantalum pentoxide (Ta_2O_5). The Greenbushes pegmatite contains significant resources of lithium, tantalum, and tin. The Greenbushes operations include a crusher and primary and secondary processing plants, which produce concentrates (Partington, McNaughton, and Williams, 1995; Global Advanced Metals Pty Ltd., 2013a).

Global Advanced Metals Pty Ltd. (GAM) has also mined tantalum at its Wodgina operation, which is located about 100 km southeast of Port Hedland in the northwestern part of Western Australia. Wodgina had a production capacity of about 250 t/yr of Ta_2O_5 from tantalum-bearing pegmatite at the Mount Cassiterite and the South Tinstone open-cut mines. The Wodgina deposit is hosted in the Archean North Pilbara Craton, which contains at least 120 pegmatites in more than 27 pegmatite groups, including the Wodgina (albite type) and the Mount Cassiterite (albite-spodumene type) pegmatites, which contain high-grade tantalum mineralization. The Wodgina processing plant produces primary tantalum concentrate grading between 8 percent and 19 percent Ta_2O_5, which is transported to

Greenbushes for secondary processing (Sweetapple and Collins, 2002; Global Advanced Metals Pty Ltd., 2013d).

Galaxy Resources Ltd. of Australia owns the Mt. Cattlin Mine, which is located about 2 km north of Ravensthorpe in Western Australia and has a production capacity of about 25 t/yr of Ta_2O_5. Tantalum ore from Mt. Cattlin is initially processed at the Greenbushes secondary processing plant (Global Advanced Metals Pty Ltd., 2013a).

In Brazil, tantalum production comes largely from the Volta Grande and the Pitinga deposits. At Volta Grande in southern Minas Gerais State, a field of large pegmatites is associated with early Proterozoic granite along the southern margin of the Archean São Francisco Craton. The pegmatites are zoned and contain abundant spodumene. The Volta Grande Mine produces ceramic feldspar, niobium, tantalum, and tin. The tantalum capacity of the Volta Grande Mine is about 25 t/yr of tantalum concentrate. At the Pitinga deposit in Central Amazonas State in northern Brazil, Paleoproterozoic volcanics of the Iricoume Group and Urupi Formation are intruded by granite plutons of the Madeira Suite, including the Madeira and the Agua Boa plutons. The granite plutons have Rapikivi and biotite granite phases as well as significant metasomatic and hydrothermal alteration. The Pintinga Mine, which is operated by Mineração Taboca S.A., has an annual capacity of about 91 t of Ta_2O_5 (180 t of tantalum concentrate). The company mines columbite ore at the mine and produces a ferroniobiumtantalum alloy that contains 45 percent niobium, 25 percent iron, and 4.2 percent tantalum and is used as a raw material in the production of niobium and tantalum oxide (Lagache and Quéméneur, 1997; Borges and others, 2009; Pohl, 2013; Mineração Taboca S.A., 2013).

The Tanco deposit, which was a leading producer of tantalum from 1969 to 1982 and has a history as a smaller producer since then, is located in southeastern Manitoba Province, Canada. At Tanco, tantalum has been produced from several zones within a pegmatite. Recently, the capacity of Tanco has been about 80 t/yr of Ta_2O_5 (Thomas and Spooner, 1988).

Central Africa—specifically Burundi, Congo (Kinshasa), and Rwanda—was the source of more than 40 percent (more than 300 t) of world primary tantalum production in 2011. In recent years, tantalum and tin have been mined from alluvial and elluvial deposits; however, in the past, lode deposits were mined. The lode deposits are principally quartz veins and pegmatites associated with a series of late- to post-orogenic granites that intrude the Kibara belt, which extends from Katanga Province and Kivu Province in Congo (Kinshasa) into parts of Burundi, Rwanda, and Tanzania, as well as Maniema Province in Congo (Kinshasa). Many of the pegmatites are thought to be small deposits; however, a large zoned pegmatite has been identified at Manono (Pohl, 1994; Kokonyangi, 2004; Dewaele and others, 2010).

The Yichun tantalum-niobium-lithium mine is hosted by a small body of topaz-lepidolite granite that is a fractionated phase of the Yashan batholith in Jiangxi Province, China. The Yichun deposit is the best known of China's tantalum deposits. In Fujian Province, the Nanping pegmatite field also hosts tantalum-niobium-tin mineralization (Yin Lin and others, 1995; Yueqing and Wenying, 1995).

In 2012, Gippsland Ltd. of Australia held 50 percent interest in the Abu Dabbab tantalum-tin deposit in joint-venture with the Egyptian Mineral Resources Co. (50 percent), which is located 770 km south of Cairo (Petra Capital Pty Ltd., 2012, p. 6). Also in 2012, resources at Abu Dabbab were estimated to be 44.5 million metric tons (Mt) at an average grade of 250 grams per metric ton (g/t) Ta_2O_5 and 90 g/t tin (Petra Capital Pty Ltd., 2012, p.12). Abu Dabbab is a fine-grained cassiterite and niobium-containing tantalite deposit hosted in altered granitic rocks. The ore zone is about 400 meters (m) long and 200 m wide and has a depth of 400 m from the maximum surface elevation (Petra Capital Pty Ltd., 2012, p. 12–13). The deposit is controlled by a northwest-trending shear zone and intersecting north-east structures. The deposit is expected to produce about 420 t of Ta_2O_5 in 2016

(Petra Capital Pty Ltd., 2012, p. 3). In 2010, Gippsland signed an offtake agreement with H.C. Starck GmbH of Germany, which included the purchase of about 300 t/yr of contained Ta_2O_5 for a period of 10 years (Petra Capital Ltd., 2012, p. 5). Each of the two companies in the joint-venture also held ownership (50 percent each) in the Nuweibi tantalum-tin-feldspar deposit. Indicated and inferred mineral resources at Nuweibi were estimated to be 98 Mt at average grades of 143 g/t Ta_2O_5 and 92 g/t niobium (Petra Capital Pty Ltd., 2012, p. 4). The company expected to produce of about 52 t of Ta_2O_5 in 2015 and 427 t of Ta_2O_5 in 2016 (Petra Capital Pty Ltd., 2012, p. 4).

The Kenticha Mine, which is operated by Ethiopian Mineral Development Share Co. (EMDSC), had an annual capacity of about 90 t of tantalum (which could produce 200 t/yr of tantalite concentrate grading 45 to 60 percent Ta_2O_5). The open pit mine is located about 550 km south of Addis Ababa and is hosted by the Kenticha pegmatite field, which is granitic pegmatite that covers an area of about 2,500 square kilometers (km^2). At Kenticha, the tantalum-bearing pegmatite deposit is exposed in an area that is more than 2 km long and 400 to 700 m wide (Mining Journal, 2011, p. 8; Geological Survey of Ethiopia, 2012, p. 3). The project produces tantalum concentrates composed of columbite-tantalite and other tantalum oxides. In February 2013, EMDSC (through its subsidiary Iris Mining Plc) and its strategic tantalum partner H.C. Starck submitted an Expression of Interest to the Privatization and Public Enterprises Supervising Agency to further develop the Kenticha Mine. Under the proposal, the companies would increase the tantalum reserves, create 12,000 jobs directly and indirectly, and produce high-end products, such as 99-percent-purity tantalum pentoxide powder and capacitor-grade tantalum powder (Business Wire, 2013). The EMDSC envisioned production of 600 t/yr of tantalite-columbite concentrate; however, no further details as to when these developments might take place were available. The company expected to add hundreds of tons of production from artisanal mines and local cooperatives (Elenilto Minerals & Mining, 2013).

Noventa Ltd. of the United Kingdom through its subsidiary Highland African Mining Co. Ltd. operated the Marropino niobium and tantalum mine, which is located about 350 km northeast of Quelimane, Zambezia Province, Mozambique. The mine had an annual production capacity of about 140 t of contained Ta_2O_5. The company's project is hosted by the Marropino pegmatite, which is a zoned lithium–rare-metal pegmatite of the lithium-cesium-tantalum family. The Marropino deposit is exposed for a strike length of about 800 m and a width of about 200 m. The company reported that there is an increase in the tantalum grade toward the center of the deposit. The known mineralization at Marropino is limited to the current area of mining and processing. As of 2010, indicated mineral resources at Marropino were estimated to be 7.40 Mt at an average grade of 223 g/t Ta_2O_5 (Hains and Mounde, 2010, p. 3, 5). In 2010, Noventa signed a 3-year offtake agreement with H.C. Starck for the sale of a substantial portion of its projected production of tantalum concentrate. During 2010, Noventa began shipment of material from the Mozambican Port of Quelimane to Nacala, Thailand, and to the United States (Noventa Ltd., 2011, p. 10, 12).

In Russia, tantalum has been mined at the Lovozerskoye deposit on the Kola Peninsula and the Etykinskoye deposit of the Zabaykalskiy mining and beneficiation complex from a massif of nepheline syenite that is enriched in elements, including beryllium, lithium, niobium, tantalum, thorium, rare-earth elements, zirconium, and volatiles, such as chlorine and fluorine. The combined capacity of these two deposits is estimated to be about 10 t/yr of tantalum ore (Smirnov, 1977).

Tantalum Processing Plants

As of 2012, at least 10 international companies were engaged in some stage of post-mining tantalum production. Tantalum refiners included Advanced Metallurgical Group N.V. of the Netherlands; GAM of Australia; H.C. Starck of Germany; and Chinese companies

Congua Tantalum & Niobium Smelter, Jiangxi Tungsten Group Limited Corp., King-Tan Tantalum Industry Ltd., and Ningxia Non-Ferrous Metal Smelter. Tantalum fabricators included Austrian companies Plansee SE and Treibacher Industrie AG; Heraeus Holding GmbH of Germany, and U.S. companies KEMET Blue Powder Corp. and Molycorp Inc.

Figure 5 shows the locations of significant tantalum fabricators and refineries. The fabricators and refineries are identified in table 3, along with each facility's annual capacity, facility type, ownership, and so forth. The numbers used to identify locations in figure 5 are keyed to the "ID" in table 3.

In January 2012, GAM completed the acquisition of the supermetals business of Cabot Corp. of Boston, Massachusetts, which included tantalum-processing plants in Boyertown, Pennsylvania, and Aizu, Japan. The company integrated the two processing plants with its existing mining and processing operations in Australia. GAM produces tantalum capacitor powders and metallurgical products at its Boyertown plant. Tantalum is often alloyed with tungsten, which improves its mechanical properties and strength but retains the fabricateability of pure tantalum. GAM's tantalum metallurgical products, which may be produced as foil, sheet, plate, wire, rod, tube, and metallurgical-grade powder, include tungsten alloy containing 2.5 percent tantalum and tungsten alloy containing 10 percent tantalum. The company's primary tantalum concentrate supply was the Wodgina Mine in northwestern Western Australia (Global Advanced Metals Pty Ltd., 2012; 2013 a–c; Roskill Information Services Ltd., 2012).

In February 2012, the capacitor manufacturer KEMET Corp. of Greenville, South Carolina, signed an agreement to acquire Niotan Inc. of Carson City, Nevada, which had been a significant supplier of tantalum powder to KEMET for several years. The Niotan tantalum fabrication facility was renamed KEMET Blue Powder. KEMET reported the acquisition to be part of its strategy to secure and stabilize its supply of tantalum raw material. In March 2012, the company also reported exclusive rights to secure raw material from Tantalite Resources of South Africa, which is a new supplier that would process conflict-free ore from the Kisenge Mine in Katanga Province in Congo (Kinshasa) (KEMET Corp., 2012a, c; Roskill Information Services Ltd., 2012).

In 2011, Molycorp Inc. of Greenwood Village, Colorado, acquired a 90 percent interest in the AS Silmet facility located in Sillamae, Estonia; this facility is one of the leading producers of tantalum metal in Europe. The processing plant manufactures tantalum hydroxides, oxides, and metals (Molycorp Inc., 2011).

King-Tan Tantalum Industry Ltd. produces tantalum bars, carbides, ingots, oxides, and powders. King-Tan, which is located in Jiangxi Province, China, sells its products to domestic and international customers, including customers in Germany, Japan, Singapore, and the United States (King-Tan Tantalum Industry Ltd., 2009a, b).

Supply Chain for Tantalum

The tantalum supply chain begins with the mining of ore and ends with the manufacture of consumer products or goods. The supply chain includes the mines, smelters, and refineries identified in figures 3, 4, and 5 and tables 1, 2, and 3 and extends downstream to include fabricators and manufacturers of intermediate and consumer goods, of which the significant ones are identified in figure 5 and table 3. Any disruption along the supply chain can result in higher prices that could affect many industries and, potentially, the availability of final goods. Identifying connections between the raw materials and the downstream entities that produce products that contain tantalum is critical to mapping the supply chain and analyzing the likelihood of supply disruption.

Sources of tantalum include artisanal mining, conventional (surface and underground) mining operations, and the recovery of tantalum from slag from tin smelting operations and from scrap recycling. Based on data from Roskill Information Services Ltd., mining operations accounted for about 74 percent of the tantalum supply in 2011, followed by 18 percent from scrap recycling and 8 percent from tin slags (Roskill Information Services Ltd., 2012). Conventional hard rock mines around the world include surface and underground mines in Australia, Brazil, Canada, and Russia. Production from Burundi, Congo (Kinshasa), and Rwanda is mostly from artisanal mining of placer deposits. After the extraction of the raw material, the ore is physically concentrated by gravity separation and then processed by a smelter and refinery to obtain refined products, which include tantalum metals, oxides, and powders. For example, portions of tantalum concentrate mined from the Kenticha, the Volta Grande (Fluminese), and the Marropino Mines were sent to H.C. Starck in Germany for refining into tantalum fabricated products, such as foils, ingots, plates, rods, sheets, and tubes, and tantalum powder and compounds, which included carbides and oxides.

Figure 6 shows examples of the relationships among selected tantalum producing mines or source materials, and processing facilities and their refined products for selected countries. Those entries for which the information given is speculative or uncertain are marked with a question mark. Figure 7 lists tantalum processing facilities in Japan along with the refined products they produce.

Tantalum Capacitors

One of the main uses of tantalum is in capacitors. Capacitors are used to store electrical charge for later use and are common to all types of electronic equipment, including that used in automobiles, cameras, computers, engine management systems, light-emitting diodes, and cell phones and other telecommunications equipment. The authors identified 25 companies engaged in the manufacture of tantalum capacitors: including Ningxia Orient Tantalum Industry Co. Ltd. of China; NEC TOKIN Corp. of Japan; Samsung Electro-Mechanics of the Republic of Korea; and U.S. companies AVX Corp., KEMET, and Vishay Intertechnology Inc. (fig. 8). As of 2012, leading tantalum capacitor producers included AVX, which accounted for about 30 percent of the total market value, KEMET, NEC TOKIN, and Vishay. AVX manufactures tantalum capacitors for automobile, aerospace, and medical applications (KEMET Corp., 2012a, c; Roskill Information Services Ltd., 2012; AVX Corp., 2013a).

Table 4 presents the location of the facilities at which AVX, KEMET, and NEC TOKIN manufacture tantalum capacitors. AVX and KEMET each have five manufacturing sites, and NEC TOKIN has seven sites. All three companies have facilities in geographically diverse areas.

AVX produces about 10 different series of capacitors, which are used in a variety of aerospace, medical, and military applications (table 5). KEMET's product list includes 85 capacitor series. Series differ based upon a number of characteristics, including composition of the capacitor, electrical characteristics, reliability, the temperature at which they will operate, and how they may be mounted in a product (table 6).

Clearly, there are a large number of manufacturers, facilities, and types of capacitors. The large number of producing companies, manufacturing facilities, and types of capacitors contributes to the complexity of estimating the probability of a disruption of the supply of final goods that contain Ta-bearing capacitors. One would need to understand the relationship between manufacturing facilites and the types of capacitors they produce to evaluate the likelihood that a disruption at a plant might disrupt production of final goods that use a particular type of capacitor. Further, one would need to know if the type of capacitor used in a particular product could be replaced by one of the many other types of capacitors. The large number of potential combinations of plants, capacitor types, and potential substitution between types of capacitors makes estimation of the probability of disruption of a supply chain at the stage of capacitor manufacture a daunting task.

Discussion and Conclusions

The present investigation of the supply chain of tantalum, although only partial with regard to the products that use or depend on tantalum, the facilities that manufacture tantalum-containing products, and which products can substitute for one another, demonstrates several important points and provides some perspectives concerning the strategies that might be employed to map supply chains. First, supply chains, when considered in their entirety (from material in the earth to the final consumer product), are incredibly complex, and reducing this complexity to a manageable level requires clearly defined questions that partition the complex supply chain into manageable parts. For example, questions about how a disruption in the supply of a key input may affect the availability of end products that use that input will be quite different than questions about what is the likelihood that a particular good could suffer a particular supply disruption. In the former case, the level of complexity at the beginning of the supply chain (mining and initial processing of mineral material) is relatively limited, as mining and mineral processing sites are relatively few and knowable. The number of final goods, their component parts, and the facilities in which they are manufactured is considerably larger, however. If supply chain disruption is approached from the end of the chain—that is, if one wants to know what is the likelihood that there will be a disruption in the availability of a particular final good—the number of final goods one must analyze is reduced but the number of initial mineral materials that must be considered will be large. Although one may limit the complexity by focusing on one part of the chain based upon the question asked, the complexity in other parts of the supply chain may not be reduced. Defining the question clearly still may not reduce some types of complexity, such as the number of particular products and the extent to which they can substitute for one another. A supply chain "map," then, must be designed to answer particular questions, and those questions will determine the level of detail that the supply chain map needs to contain to answer the questions. This is very much analogous to the approach used with topographic and geologic maps, which, depending on the scale of the map, contain more or less detail about land forms and geology of the mapped entity. To determine the likelihood that the supply chain of a particular product could be disrupted, a very detailed analysis of the supply chain involving all materials and their subsequent transformations and potential substitutes is necessary. Such an analysis is expensive to perform and can become obsolete if part of the production process for that good changes, and so, a detailed map of a supply chain is usually not available. The question then becomes at what 'scale' a supply chain map can be prepared that will be of use in evaluating the vulnerability of supply chain disruption without fully mapping the chain.

In the case of tantalum, there are a few mines that produce tantalum minerals; however, those mines supply several processing facilities, directly or through traders. Refined mineral products are further processed to make chemicals, metals (or alloys), or simply a more-refined mineral (that is, greater purity and (or) more controlled physical properties, such as particle size). Metals and chemicals can go through several steps while being incorporated into a product, and the number of facilities involved often increases. So, tantalum starts with a few facilities (mines), passes through a complex web of facilities, and then becomes incorporated in a large number of products. The increasing number of facilities, material paths, and buyer-seller needs (as they relate to material requirements) result in greater complexity as one moves down the supply chain from mining to consumer product.

At some point in the supply chain, material requirements are replaced by performance criteria, which further complicates analysis. Take, for example, the large number of tantalum capacitors described in the capacitor section of this report. Looking backwards through the supply chain (that is, from product to material source) is a useful way to analyze risk. Bear in mind, however, that not all supply paths are connected or overlap. Materials in the early part of the supply chain (for example, minerals) have more possible uses than materials at the end of the supply chain (for example, cell phones and turbine engines). As a result, a supply disruption at the beginning of the supply chain can have a broader effect as material changes paths among processing facilities than would a supply disruption at the downstream end of the supply chain. On the other hand, a downstream interruption affects fewer products. It is possible that certain products depend on materials that follow a path through one facility, making that facility critical to that product; that is, a "pinch point" in the supply chain.

Many supply chain maps produced to date have focused on the front end of the chain; that is, the extraction of mineral materials and their initial processing, and provide a list of final goods that may contain those materials (European Commission Enterprise and Industry Directorate, 2010). Such an approach typically focuses on the degree of concentration of the production of mineral materials. This is useful for identifying those materials that are more likely to be subject to disruption. These maps, however, provide only very general information about the downstream parts of the supply chain. What is needed is information that could be applied to a number of different end products. One such approach would be to gather information on key technologies that are used in a large number of final goods. This approach still entails considerable work as the situation with tantalum-containing capacitors demonstrates. It can, however, provide information on the downstream parts of the supply chains of a large number of final goods. It can also map which products are connected to which mines through which processing facilities.

Another issue is how best to present information about material flow that is useful in identifying risk and is understandable. In this report, maps show geographic facility location and charts show connections between producers and in the supply chain that may be linked by ownership, investment connection, and (or) purchase contracts.

Other factors that contribute to supply risk but that are not included in this report are commercial infrastructure (for example, competent manpower, electrical power supply, and transportation) and good governance (for example, the legal infrastructure and the business friendly nature of the geographic area).

References Cited

AVX Corp., 2013a, AVX Categories—Capacitors—Tantalum: Fountain Inn, South Carolina, AVX Corp. (Accessed May 17, 2013, at http://www.avx.com/prodinfo_catlist.asp?ParentID=48.)

AVX Corp., 2013b, AVX tantalum: Fountain Inn, South Carolina, AVX Corp., May, 3 p. (Accessed June 25, 2013, at http://www.avx.com/docs/Catalogs/tantintr.pdf.)

Borges, R.M.K., Villas, R.N.N., Fuzikawa, K., Dall'Agnol, R., Pimenta, M.A., 2009, Phase separation, fluid mixing, and origin of the greisens and potassic episyenite associated with the Água Boa pluton, Pitinga tin province, Amazonian Craton, Brazil: Journal of South American Earth Sciences, v. 27, issue 2–3, February, p. 161–183.

British Geological Survey, 2011, Niobium-tantalum: Nottingham, United Kingdom, British Geological Survey, April, 27 p. (Accessed August 7, 2013, at http://www.bgs.ac.uk/downloads/start.cfm?id=2033.)

Business Wire, 2013, Elenilto & H.C. Starck bid to develop the Kenticha's tantalum mine: London, United Kingdom, Business Wire, February 18. (Accessed March 17, 2013, at http://www.businesswire.com/news/home/20130218005545/en/Elenilto-H.C.-Starck-Bid-Develop-Kenticha%E2%80%99s-Tantalum.)

Dewaele, S., De Clercq, F., Muchez, P., Schneider, J., Burgess, R., Boyce, A., and Fernandez-Alonso, M., 2010, Geology of the cassiterite mineralization in the Rutongo area, Rwanda (Central Africa)—Current state of knowledge: Geologica Belgica, v. 13, issue 1–2, p. 91–112.

Elenilto Minerals & Mining, 2013, Ethiopia—Kenticha tantalum project: London, United Kingdom, Elenilto Minerals & Mining. (Accessed March 17, 2013, at http://www.elenilto.com/projects/tantalum-niobium/ethiopia-bupo-kilkile/.)

European Commission Enterprise and Industry Directorate, 2010, Critical raw materials for the EU—Report of the ad-hoc working group on defining critical raw materials: European Commission, July 30, 85 p. (Accessed June 20, 2013, at http://ec.europa.eu/enterprise/policies/raw-materials/files/docs/report-b_en.pdf.)

Geological Survey of Ethiopia, 2012, Tantalum—Key mineral for gadgets and electronic equipment: Addis Ababa, Ethiopia, Geological Survey of Ethiopia, January, 4 p. (Accessed August 7, 2013, at http://extra.geus.info/cet/ethiopia/EthiopienBlad_TANTALUM.pdf.)

Global Advanced Metals Pty Ltd., 2012, Acquisition of Cabot Supermetals completed: West Perth, Western Australia, Australia, Global Advanced Metals Pty Ltd. media release, January 23, 2 p. (Accessed April 16, 2013, at http://www.globaladvancedmetals.com/media/29722/supermetals acquisition completed 23 jan 2012.pdf.)

Global Advanced Metals Pty Ltd., 2013a, Greenbushes—Australia: Global Advanced Metals Pty Ltd. (Accessed June 17, 2013, at http://www.globaladvancedmetals.com/our-operations/gam-resources/greenbushes-australia.aspx.)

Global Advanced Metals Pty Ltd., 2013b, Tantalum concentrate: Global Advanced Metals Pty Ltd. (Accessed April 16, 2013, at http://www.globaladvancedmetals.com/our-products/tantalum-concentrate.aspx.)

Global Advanced Metals Pty Ltd., 2013c, Tantalum metallurgical products: Global Advanced Metals Pty Ltd. (Accessed April 16, 2013, at http://www.globaladvancedmetals.com/our-products/tantalum-metallurgical-products.aspx.)

Global Advanced Metals Pty Ltd., 2013d, Wodgina—Australia: Global Advanced Metals Pty Ltd. (Accessed April 16, 2013, at http://www.globaladvancedmetals.com/our-operations/gam-resources/wodgina-australia.aspx.)

Hains, D.H., and Mounde, Mark, 2010, Technical report on the Marropino project and associated properties, Zambezia Province, Mozambique—NI 43–101 technical report, prepared for Noventa Ltd.: Toronto, Ontario, Canada, Scott Wilson Roscoe Postle Associates Inc., 197 p. plus 3 appendixes. (Accessed June 13, 2013, at http://www.noventagroup.com/wp-content/uploads/pdf/SW_43-101_Noventa-Report-Oct-15-2010.pdf.)

KEMET Corp., 2012a, KEMET Blue Powder Corporation meets all conflict-free smelter site requirements: Greenville, South Carolina, KEMET Corp., March 1. (Accessed April 12, 2013, at http://www.kemet.com/page/new2012512.)

KEMET Corp., 2012b, KEMET signs agreement to acquire 34% interest in NEC TOKIN—Option to acquire 100% ownership: Greenville, South Carolina, KEMET Corp., March 12. (Accessed July 25, 2013, at http://www.kemet.com/page/new2012515.)

KEMET Corp., 2012c, KEMET signs agreement to acquire Niotan Incorporated: Greenville, South Carolina, KEMET Corp., February 2, 1 p. (Accessed April 9, 2013, at http://www.kemet.com/page/new2012504.)

KEMET Corp., 2012d, Setting the course for success—Annual report 2012: Simpsonville, South Carolina, KEMET Corp., 141 p. (Accessed June 25, 2013, at http://b2icontent.irpass.cc/2072%2F137048.pdf?AWSAccessKeyId=1Y51NDPSZK99KT3F8VG2&Expires=1372271139&Signature=Jc%2FVrd4kvts7dffcaeMJ2g1VbG4%3D.)

KEMET Corp., 2013a, Product selection guide: Simpsonville, South Carolina, KEMET Corp., 64 p. (Accessed May 17, 2013, at http://www.kemet.com/kemet/web/homepage/kechome.nsf/file/2013_Product_Selection_Guide/$file/ 2013_Product_Selection_Guide.pdf.)

KEMET Corp., 2013b, Tantalum capacitors: Simpsonville, South Carolina, KEMET Corp. (Accessed August 9, 2013, *at* http://www.kemet.com/kemet/web/homepage/kechome.nsf/weben/ Tantalum *Capacitors.)*

King-Tan Tantalum Industry Ltd., 2009a, Product list: Yifeng, Jiangxi, China, King-Tan Tantalum Industry Ltd. (Accessed April 17, 2013, at http://www.king-tan.com/products_list.html.)

King-Tan Tantalum Industry Ltd., 2009b, Sales: Yifeng, Jiangxi, China, King-Tan Tantalum Industry Ltd. (Accessed April 17, 2013, at http://www.king-tan.com/comcontent_detail/ &FrontComContent_list01-001CurrentIds=08f3375a-fdb0-4462-a221-ad36b003da35__9fd56bec-d07d-4f85-aa15-f3b3fedaa80e&comContentId=9fd56bec-d07d-4f85-aa15-f3b3fedaa80e&comp_stats=comp-FrontComContent_list01-001.html.*)*

Kokonyangi, 2004, Structural constraints on cassiterite and colombite-tantalite mineralization in the Kibaran belt, D.R. Congo (Central Africa)—Implication for the timing of ore formation: Journal of Geoscience, v. 47, no. 11, March, p.127–140.

Kuo, C.S., 2013, The mineral industry of Mozambique, *in* Area reports—International—Asia and the Pacific: U.S. Geological Survey Minerals Yearbook 2011, v. III, p. 13.1–13.13.

Lagache, Martine, and Quéméneur, Joël, 1997, The Volta Grande pegmatites, Minas Gerais, Brazil—An example of rare-element granitic pegmatites exceptionally enriched in lithium and rubidium: The Canadian Mineralogist, v. 35, p. 135–165.

Menzie, W.D., Baker, M.S., Bleiwas, D.I., and Kuo, Chin, 2011, Mines and mineral processing facilities in the vicinity of the March 11, 2011, earthquake in northern Honshu, Japan: U.S. Geological Survey Open-File Report 2011–1069, 7 p. (Accessed June 20, 2013, at http://pubs.usgs.gov/of/2011/1069/.)

Mineração Taboca S.A., 2013, Products—Ferro-niobium-tantalum alloy (FeNbTa): Mineração Taboca S.A. (Accessed May 8, 2013, at http://www.mtaboca.com.br/eng/produtos/liga.asp.)

Mining Journal, 2011, Ethiopia—A supplement to Mining Journal: London, United Kingdom, Mining Journal special edition, January, 15 p. (Accessed March 25, 2013, at http://www.mining-journal.com/ __data/assets/supplement_file_attachment/0018/251217/Ethiopia_scr.pdf.)

Mobbs, P.M., 2012, The mineral industry of Nigeria, *in* Area reports—International—Africa and Middle East: U.S. Geological Survey Minerals Yearbook 2011, v. III, p. 33.1–33.4.

Molycorp Inc., 2011, Molycorp acquires controlling stake in AS Silmet, expands operations to Europe, doubles near-term rare earth oxide production capacity: Greenwood Village, Colorado, and Tallin, Estonia, Molycorp Inc. news release, April 4. (Accessed April 12, 2013, at http://www.molycorp.com/molycorp-acquires-controlling-stake-in-as-silmet-expands-operations-to-europe-doubles-near-term-rare-earth-oxide-production-capacity-2.)

Naughton, Keith, 2011, Ford curbs black, red paint use amid Japan quake shortage: Bloomberg L.P., March 24. (Accessed June 20, 2013, at http://www.bloomberg.com/news/2011-03-24/ ford-limits-use-of-black-red-paints-amid-japan-quake-shortage.html.)

NEC TOKIN Corp., 2013, Domestic network: NEC TOKIN Corp. (Accessed June 25, 2013, at http://www.nec-tokin.com/english/info/network.html.)

Noventa Ltd., 2011, Annual report and financial statements 2010: Saint Helier, Jersey [United Kingdom], Noventa Ltd., February 3, 96 p. (Accessed March 25, 2013, at http://www.noventagroup.com/wp-content/uploads/pdf/04022011-Noventa-RA-2010.pdf.)

Papp, J.F., 2009, Tantalum: U.S. Geological Survey Mineral Commodity Summaries 2009, p. 164–165.

Papp, J.F., 2010, Tantalum: U.S. Geological Survey Mineral Commodity Summaries 2010, p. 162–163.

Papp, J.F., 2011, Tantalum: U.S. Geological Survey Mineral Commodity Summaries 2011, p. 162–163.

Papp, J.F., 2012a, Niobium (columbium) and tantalum, in Metals and minerals: U.S. Geological Survey Minerals Yearbook 2011, v. I, p. 52.1–52.14. (Accessed July 30, 2013, at http://minerals.usgs.gov/minerals/pubs/commodity/niobium/myb1-2011-niobi.pdf.)

Papp, J.F., 2012b, Tantalum: U.S. Geological Survey Mineral Commodity Summaries 2012, p. 162–163.

Papp, J.F., 2013, Tantalum: U.S. Geological Survey Mineral Commodity Summaries 2013, p. 162–163.

Partington, G.A., McNaughton, N.J., and Williams, I.S., 1995, A review of the geology, mineralization, and geochronology of the Greenbushes pegmatite, Western Australia: Economic Geology, v. 90, issue 3, p. 616–635.

Petra Capital Pty Ltd., 2012, Gippsland Ltd.—Emerging "tier 1" tantalum-tin producer: Sydney, New South Wales, Australia, Petra Capital Pty Ltd., 20 p. plus 4 appendixes.

Pohl, W.L., 1994, Metallogeny of the northeastern Kibara belt, Central Africa—Recent perspectives: Ore Geology Reviews, v. 9, no. 2, p. 105–130. DOI: http://dx.doi.org/10.1016/0169-1368(94)90024-8.

Pohl, W.L., 2013, Economic geology of metals, chap. 2 of Economic geology, principles and practice— Metals, minerals, coal and hydrocarbons—An introduction to formation and sustainable exploration of mineral deposits: Oxford, United Kingdom, Wiley-Blackwell, 680 p. (Accessed July 25, 2013, via http://onlinelibrary.wiley.com/doi/10.1002/9781444394870/.) DOI: http://dx.doi.org/10.1002/9781444394870

Roskill Information Services Ltd., 2012, Tantalum—Market outlook to 2016: London, United Kingdom, Roskill Information Services Ltd., 164 p.

Smirnov, V.I.,ed., 1977, Ore deposits of the USSR: London, United Kingdom, Pitman Publishing Ltd., v. III, 492 p.

Sweetapple, M.T., and Collins, P.L.F., 2002, Genetic framework for the classification and distribution of Archean rare metal pegmatites in the North Pilbara Craton, Western Australia, Economic Geology, v. 97, no. 4, p. 873–895. DOI: http://dx.doi.org/10.2113/gsecongeo.97.4.873.

Tantalum-Niobium International Study Center, 2013, Tantalum—Raw materials and processing: Tantalum-Niobium International Study Center. (Accessed September 25, 2013, at http://tanb.org/tantalum.)

Thomas, A.V., and Spooner, E.T.C., 1988, Occurrence, petrology and fluid inclusion characteristics of tantalum mineralization in the Tanco granitic pegmatite southeastern Manitoba, in Taylor R.P., and Strong D.F., Recent advances in the geology of granite-related mineral deposits: Montreal, Quebec, Canada, Canadian Institute of Mining and Metallurgy, v. 39, p. 208–221.

Tse, Pui-Kwan, 2013, The mineral industry of China, in Area reports—International—Asia and the Pacific: U.S. Geological Survey Minerals Yearbook 2011, v. III, p. 9.1–9.27.

Yager, T.R., 2013a, The mineral industry of Congo (Kinshasa), in Area reports—International—Africa and Middle East: U.S. Geological Survey Minerals Yearbook 2011, v. III, p. 11.1–11.9.

Yager, T.R., 2013b, The mineral industry of Mozambique, in Area reports—International—Africa and Middle East: U.S. Geological Survey Minerals Yearbook 2011, v. III, p. 31.1—31.6.

Yager, T.R., 2013c, The mineral industry of Rwanda, in Area reports—International—Africa and Middle East: U.S. Geological Survey Minerals Yearbook 2011, v. III, p. 34.1–34.4.

Yin Lin, Pollard, P.J., Shouxi, Hu, and Taylor, R.G., 1995, Geologic and geochemical characteristics of the Yichun Ta-Nb-Li deposit, Jiangxi Province, South China: Economic Geology and the Bulletin of the Society of Economic Geologists, v. 90, no. 3, p. 577–585.
DOI: http://dx.doi.org/10.2113/gsecongeo.90.3.577.

Yueqing, Yang, and Wenying, Wang., 1995, Ta-Nb-Sn mineralization in the Nanping granitic pegmatite, Fujian, China, *in* Wang, Sijing, Scientia Geologica Sinica: Beijing, China, Science Press, v. 4, no. 2, p. 193–209.

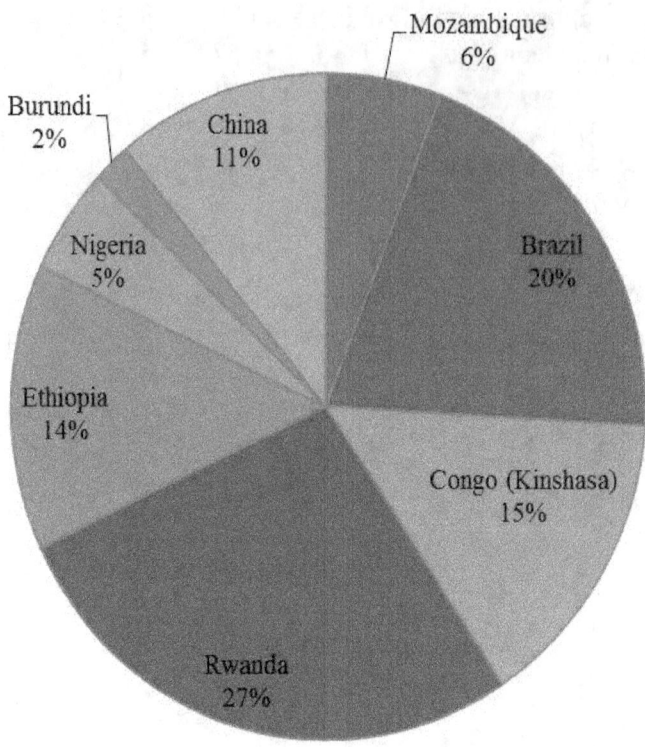

Figure 1. Chart showing percentage of mined tantalum produced in the world in 2011, by country. The amount of contained tantalum in the ore totaled 706 metric tons. Data are from Mobbs (2012), Papp (2013), Tse (2013), and Yager (2013a–c).

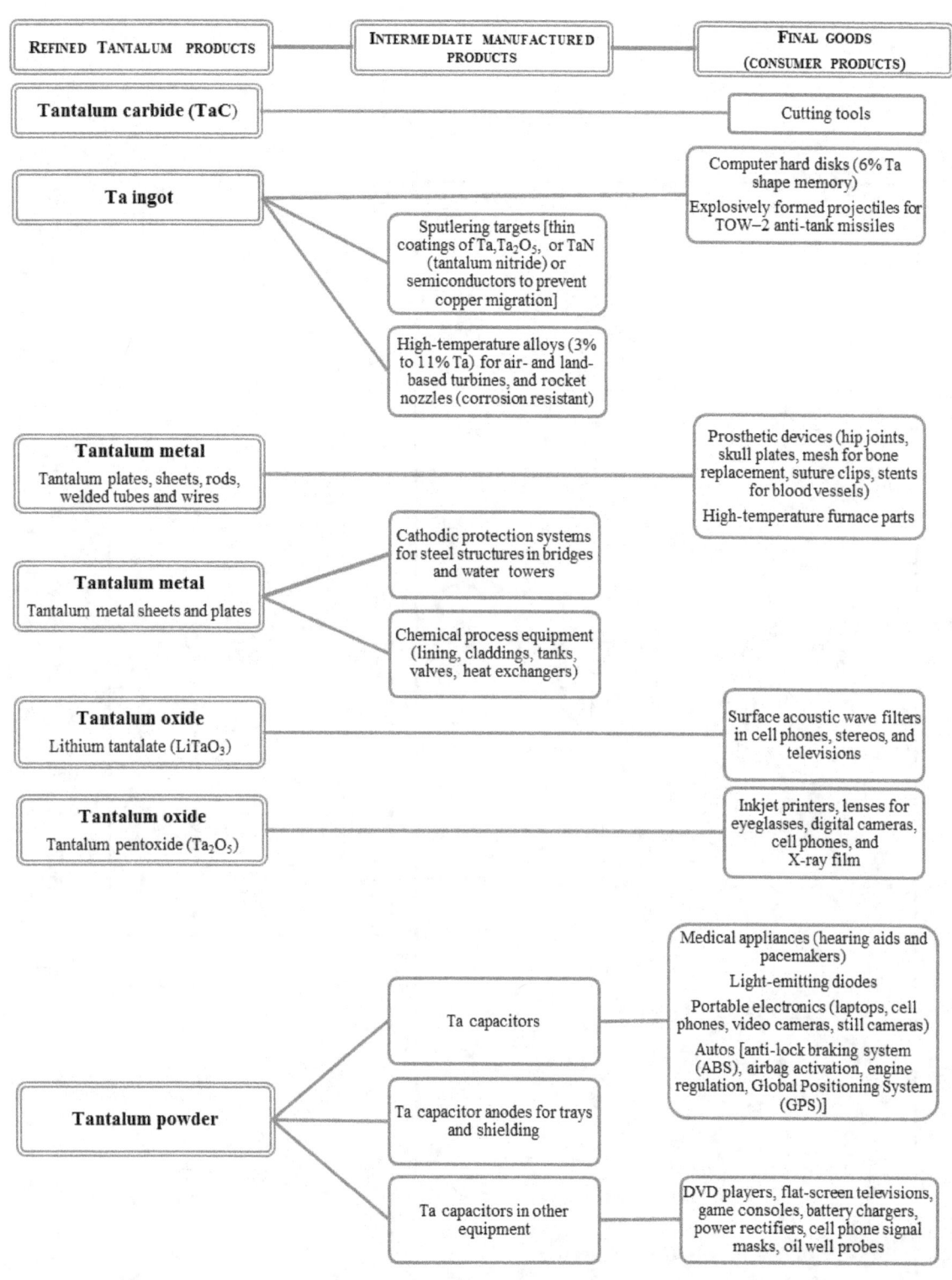

REFINED TANTALUM PRODUCTS	INTERMEDIATE MANUFACTURED PRODUCTS	FINAL GOODS (CONSUMER PRODUCTS)

Tantalum carbide (TaC) → Cutting tools

Ta ingot
- Computer hard disks (6% Ta shape memory)
- Explosively formed projectiles for TOW–2 anti-tank missiles
- Sputtering targets [thin coatings of Ta,Ta₂O₅, or TaN (tantalum nitride) or semiconductors to prevent copper migration]
- High-temperature alloys (3% to 11% Ta) for air- and land-based turbines, and rocket nozzles (corrosion resistant)

Tantalum metal
Tantalum plates, sheets, rods, welded tubes and wires
- Prosthetic devices (hip joints, skull plates, mesh for bone replacement, suture clips, stents for blood vessels)
- High-temperature furnace parts

Tantalum metal
Tantalum metal sheets and plates
- Cathodic protection systems for steel structures in bridges and water towers
- Chemical process equipment (lining, claddings, tanks, valves, heat exchangers)

Tantalum oxide
Lithium tantalate (LiTaO₃)
- Surface acoustic wave filters in cell phones, stereos, and televisions

Tantalum oxide
Tantalum pentoxide (Ta₂O₅)
- Inkjet printers, lenses for eyeglasses, digital cameras, cell phones, and X-ray film

Tantalum powder
- Ta capacitors
  - Medical appliances (hearing aids and pacemakers)
  - Light-emitting diodes
  - Portable electronics (laptops, cell phones, video cameras, still cameras)
  - Autos [anti-lock braking system (ABS), airbag activation, engine regulation, Global Positioning System (GPS)]
- Ta capacitor anodes for trays and shielding
- Ta capacitors in other equipment
  - DVD players, flat-screen televisions, game consoles, battery chargers, power rectifiers, cell phone signal masks, oil well probes

Figure 2. Chart showing refined tantalum (Ta) products, intermediate products manufactured from them, and the final goods produced (British Geological Survey, 2011; Tantalum-Niobium International Study Center, 2013).

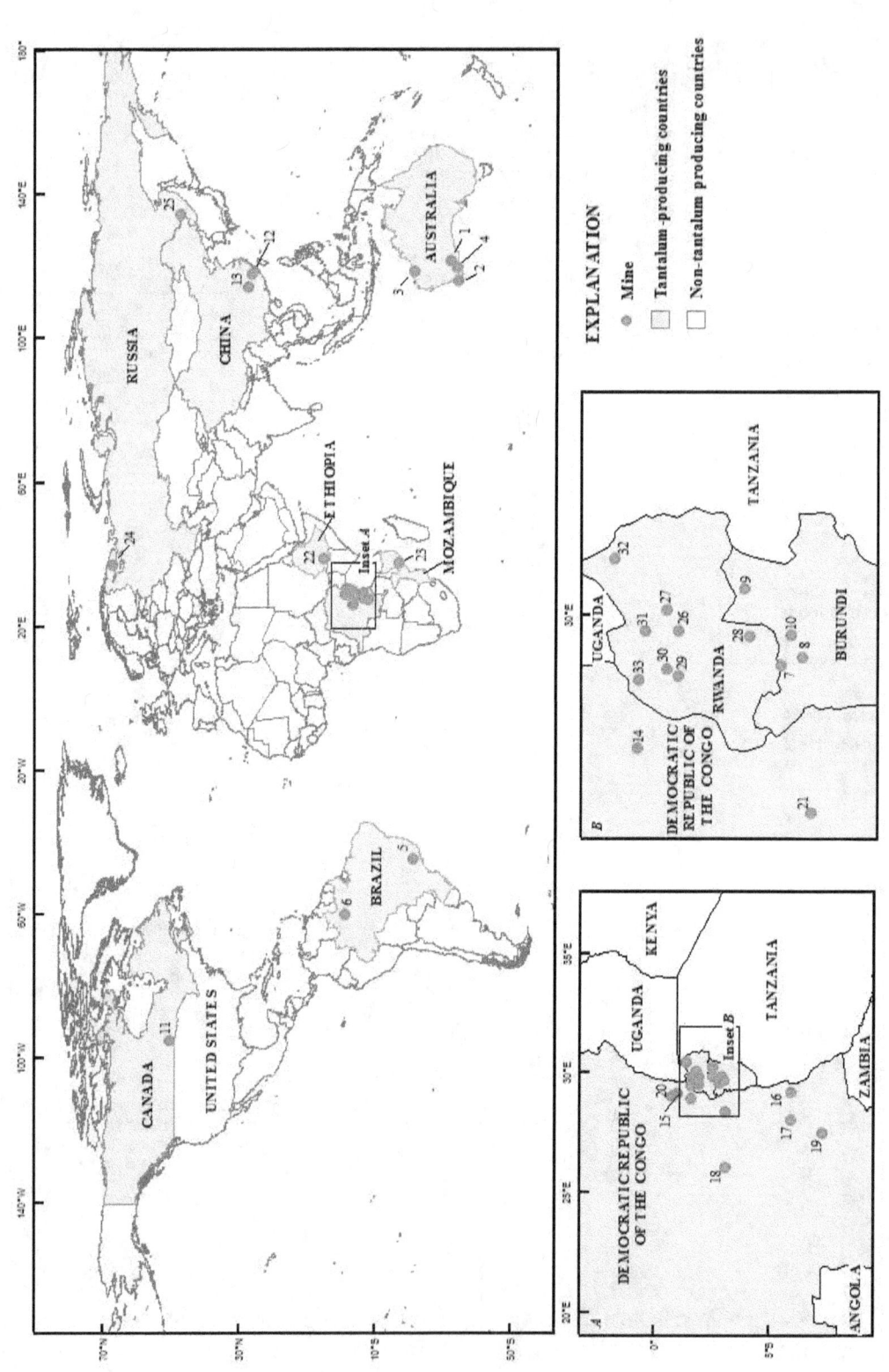

Figure 3. Significant tantalum (Ta) mines in the world. Insets *A* an *B* show the location of Ta mines in Burundi, the Democratic Republic of the Congo [Congo (Kinshasa)], and Rwanda in detail. The numbers used to identify locations are keyed to the "ID" in table 1.

16

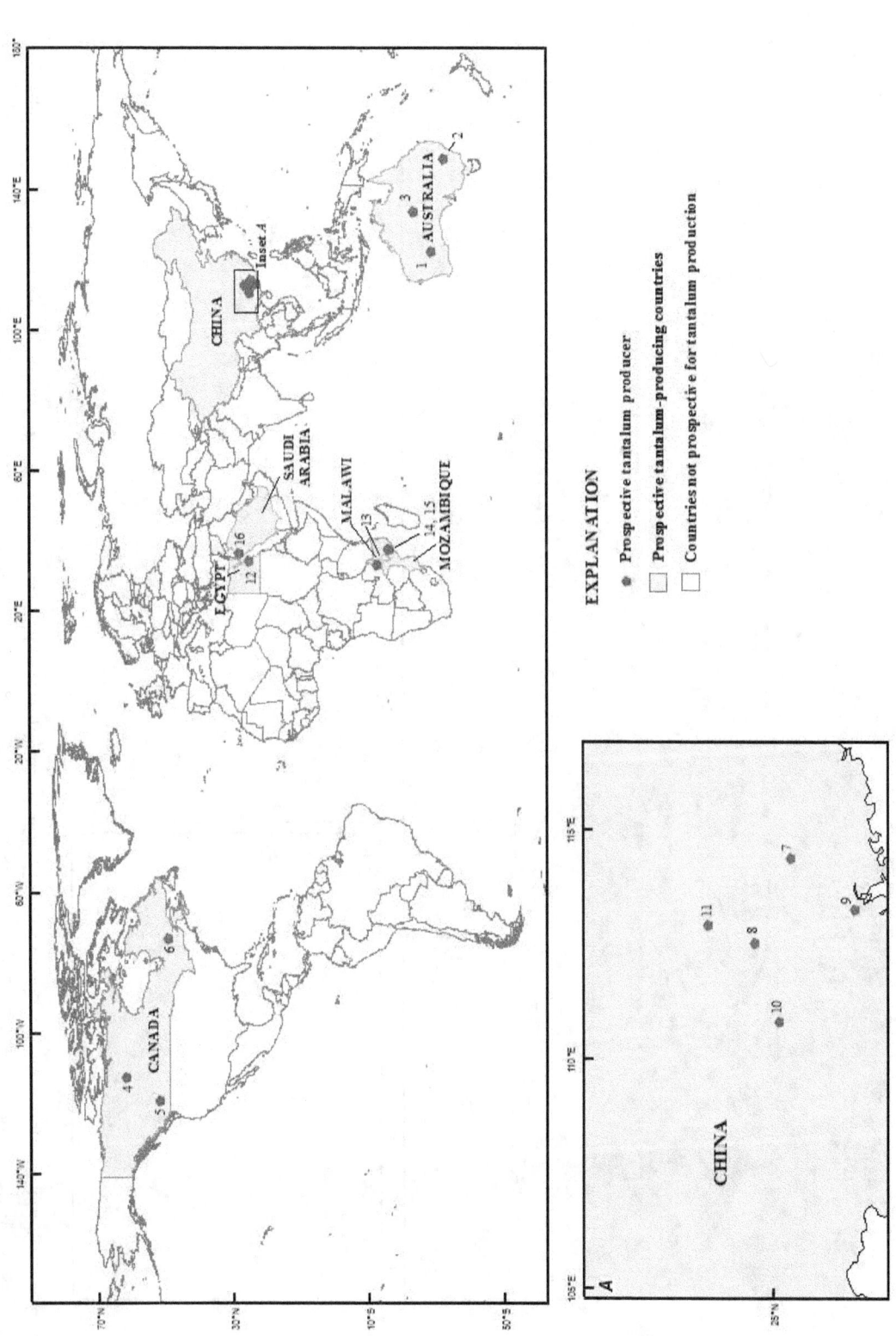

Figure 4. Prospective tantalum (Ta) producers in the world. Inset *A* shows the locations of prospective producers in China in detail. The numbers used to identify locations are keyed to the "ID" in table 2.

17

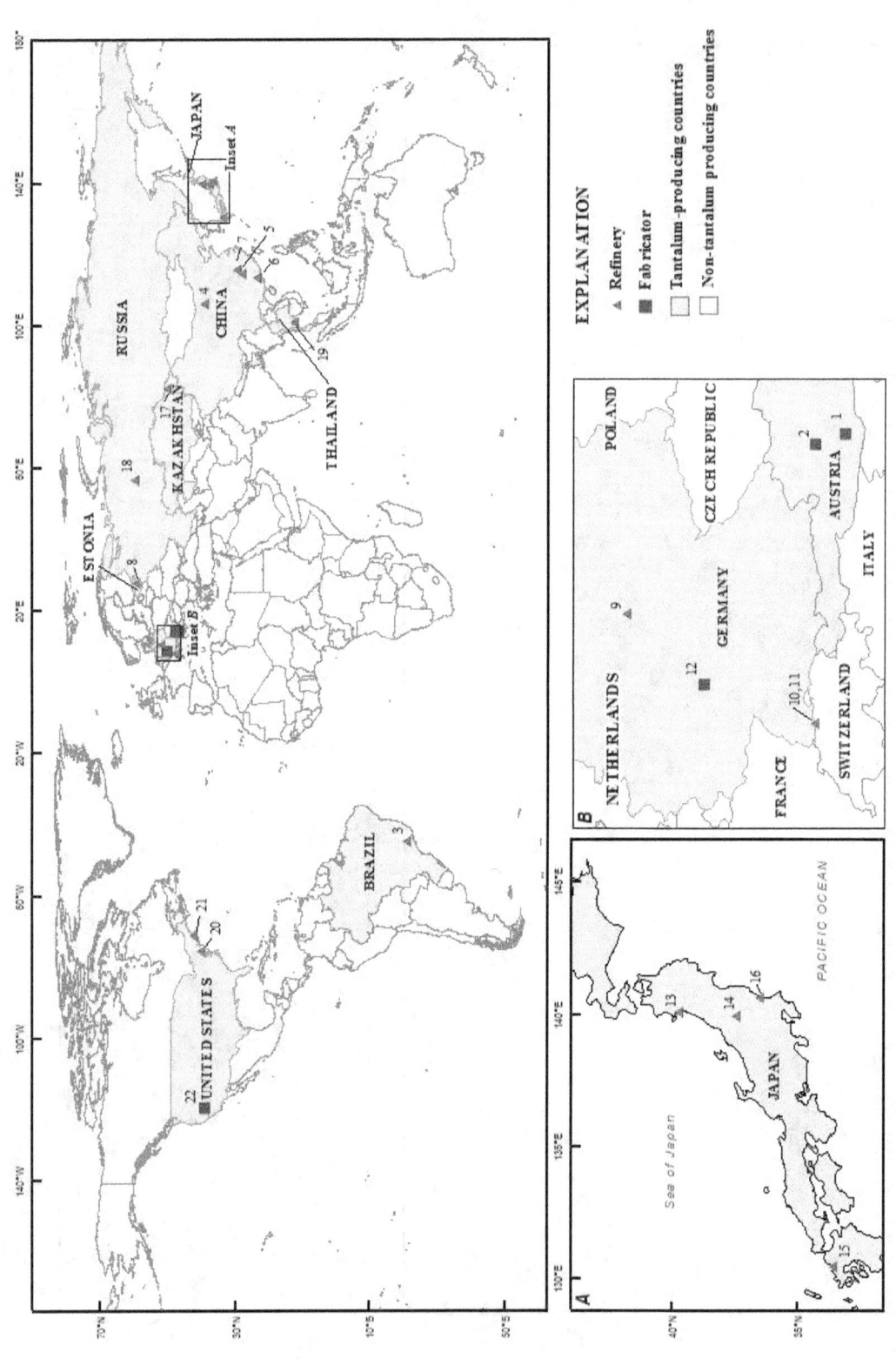

Figure 5. Significant tantalum (Ta) fabricators and refineries in the world. Inset A shows the locations of Ta refineries in Japan in detail. Inset B shows the locations of Ta fabricators and refineries in Austria and Germany in detail. The numbers used to identify locations are keyed to the "ID" in table 3.

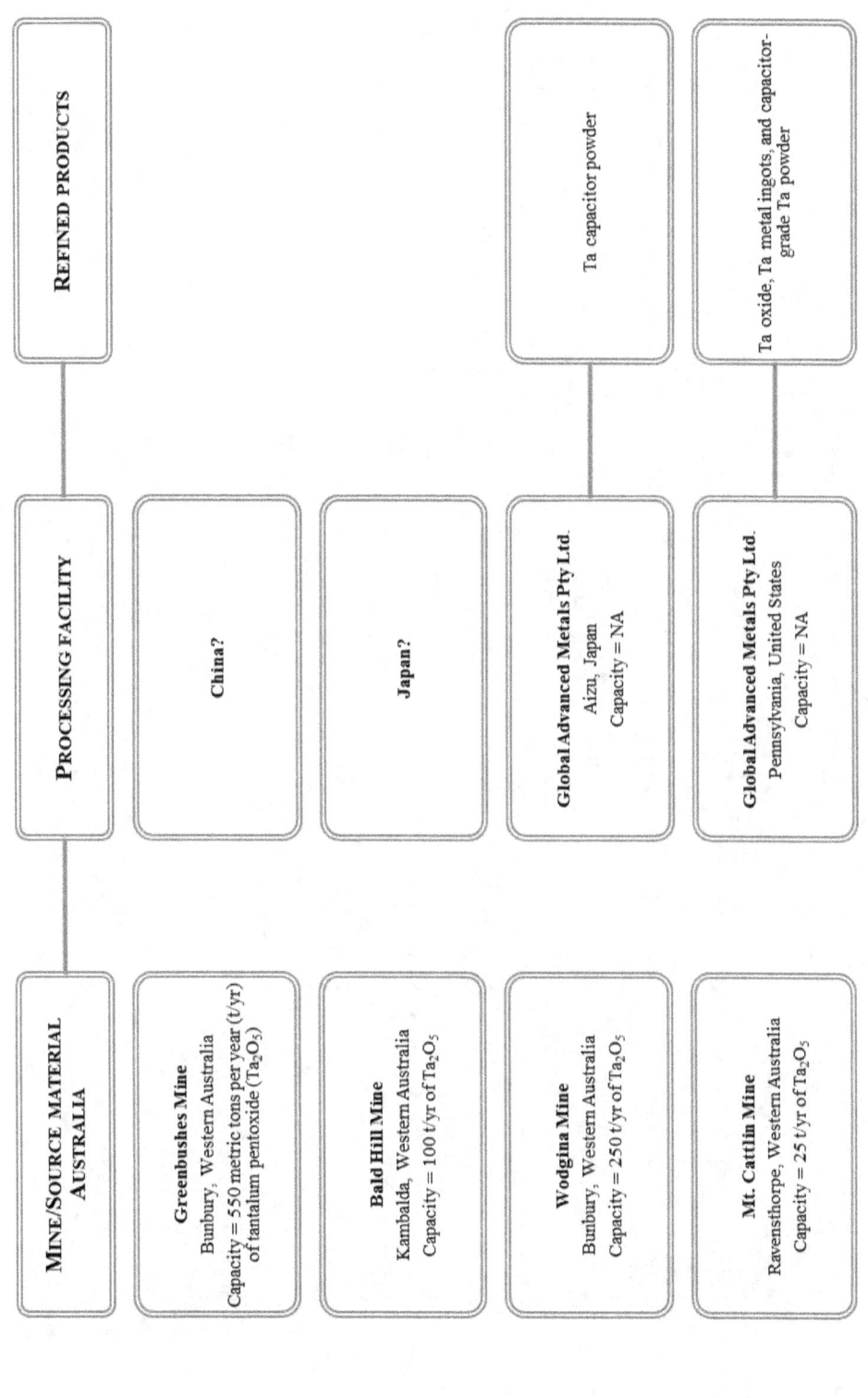

Figure 6. Chart showing the relationship of selected tantalum (Ta) mines (or source materials) and processing facilities and their refined products for mines or deposits located in A, Australia; B, Brazil; C, Burundi; D, Canada; E, China; F, Democratic Republic of the Congo [Congo (Kinshasa)]; G, Egypt; H, Ethiopia; I, Mozambique; J, Thailand; K, Russia; and L, Rwanda. A question mark after the entry indicates a probable location. Abbreviations for compounds and other terms are defined at first use in the figure. For Burundi, * indicates combined capacity. For Thailand, the Ta production capacity was estimated based on tin slag smelting operations in the country.

19

B

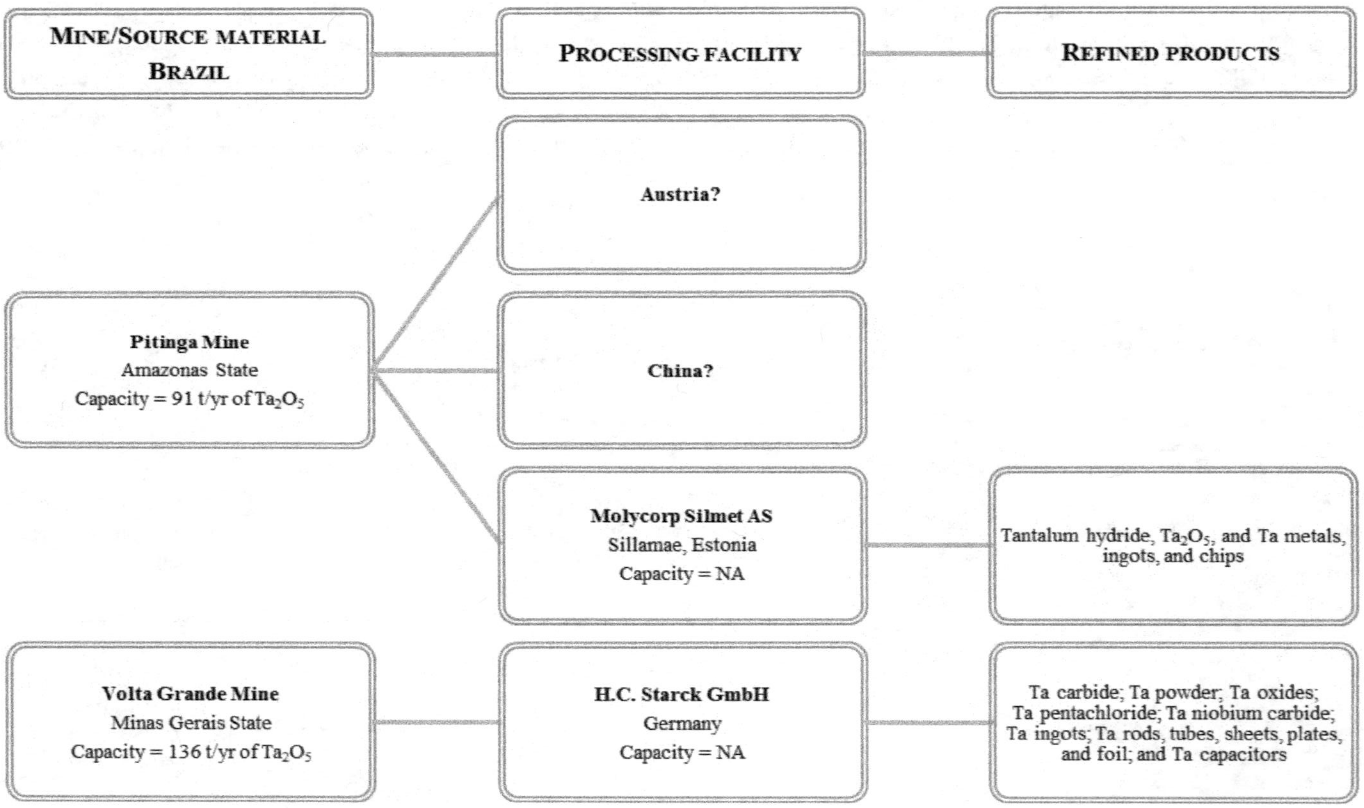

| MINE/SOURCE MATERIAL BRAZIL | PROCESSING FACILITY | REFINED PRODUCTS |

Pitinga Mine
Amazonas State
Capacity = 91 t/yr of Ta$_2$O$_5$

Volta Grande Mine
Minas Gerais State
Capacity = 136 t/yr of Ta$_2$O$_5$

Austria?

China?

Molycorp Silmet AS
Sillamae, Estonia
Capacity = NA

H.C. Starck GmbH
Germany
Capacity = NA

Tantalum hydride; Ta$_2$O$_5$; and Ta metals, ingots, and chips

Ta carbide; Ta powder; Ta oxides; Ta pentachloride; Ta niobium carbide; Ta ingots; Ta rods, tubes, sheets, plates, and foil; and Ta capacitors

20

Figure 6.—Continued

MINE/SOURCE MATERIAL
BURUNDI

Mine at Kabarore

Kabarore, Kayanza Province

Estimated capacity = 6 t/yr of columbium (Nb), Ta, and columbite-tantalite ore and concentrate

Mines at Kayanza Province*

Kayanza Province

Estimated capacity = 160 t/yr of Nb, Ta, and columbite-tantalite ore and concentrate

Mines at Kirundo Province*

Kirundo Province

Estimated capacity = 160 t/yr of Nb, Ta, and columbite-tantalite ore and concentrate

Mines at Ngozi Province*

Ngozi Province

Estimated capacity = 160 t/yr of Nb, Ta, and columbite-tantalite ore and concentrate

C

21

Figure 6.—Continued

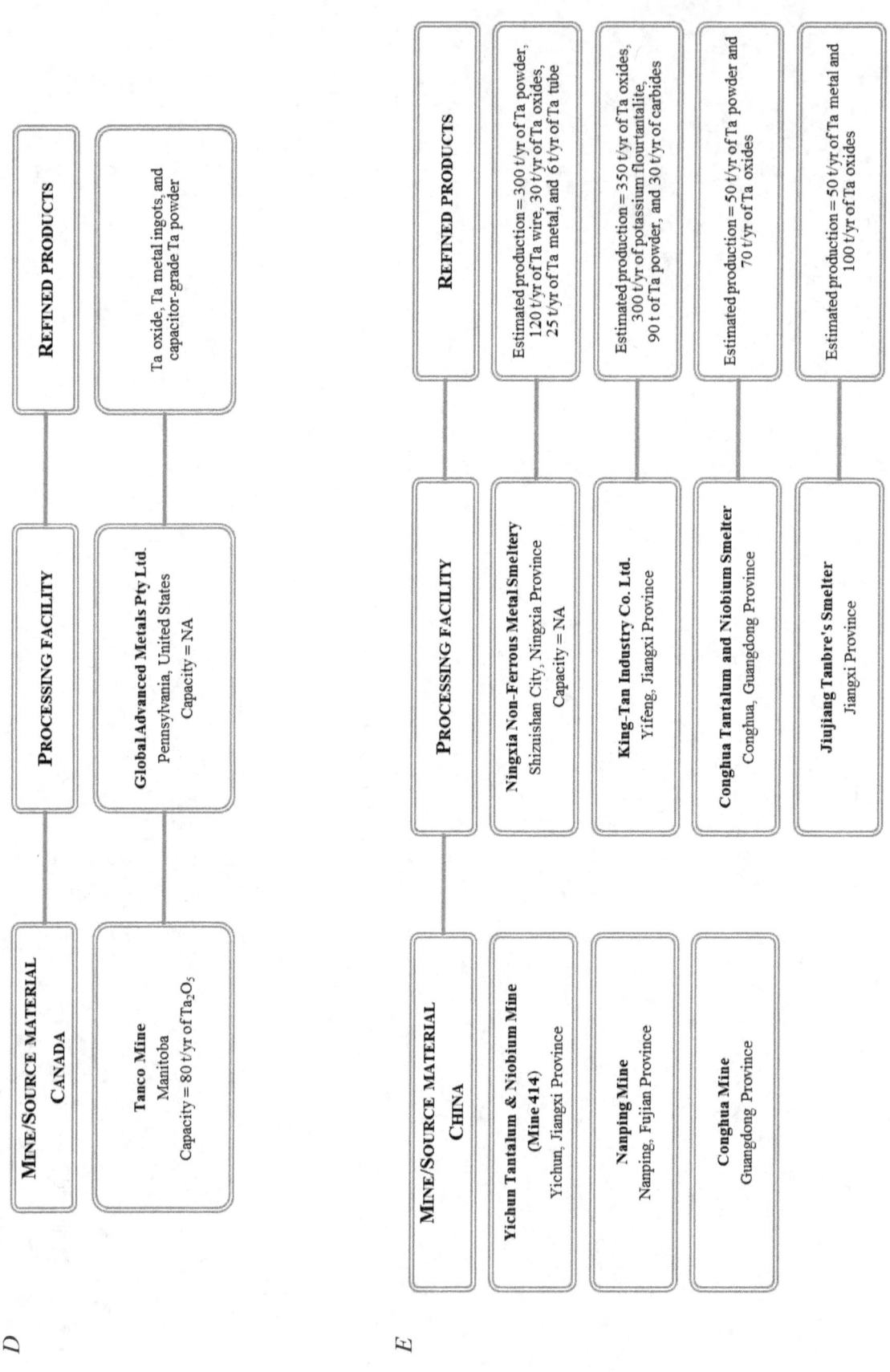

D

MINE/SOURCE MATERIAL CANADA	PROCESSING FACILITY	REFINED PRODUCTS
Tanco Mine Manitoba Capacity = 80 t/yr of Ta₂O₅	**Global Advanced Metals Pty Ltd.** Pennsylvania, United States Capacity = NA	Ta oxide, Ta metal ingots, and capacitor-grade Ta powder

E

MINE/SOURCE MATERIAL CHINA	PROCESSING FACILITY	REFINED PRODUCTS
Yichun Tantalum & Niobium Mine (Mine 414) Yichun, Jiangxi Province	**Ningxia Non-Ferrous Metal Smeltery** Shizuishan City, Ningxia Province Capacity = NA	Estimated production = 300 t/yr of Ta powder, 120 t/yr of Ta wire, 30 t/yr of Ta oxides, 25 t/yr of Ta metal, and 6 t/yr of Ta tube
Nanping Mine Nanping, Fujian Province	**King-Tan Industry Co. Ltd.** Yifeng, Jiangxi Province	Estimated production = 350 t/yr of Ta oxides, 300 t/yr of potassium flourtantalite, 90 t of Ta powder, and 30 t/yr of carbides
Conghua Mine Guangdong Province	**Conghua Tantalum and Niobium Smelter** Conghua, Guangdong Province	Estimated production = 50 t/yr of Ta powder and 70 t/yr of Ta oxides
	Jiujiang Tanbre's Smelter Jiangxi Province	Estimated production = 50 t/yr of Ta metal and 100 t/yr of Ta oxides

Figure 6.—Continued

22

F

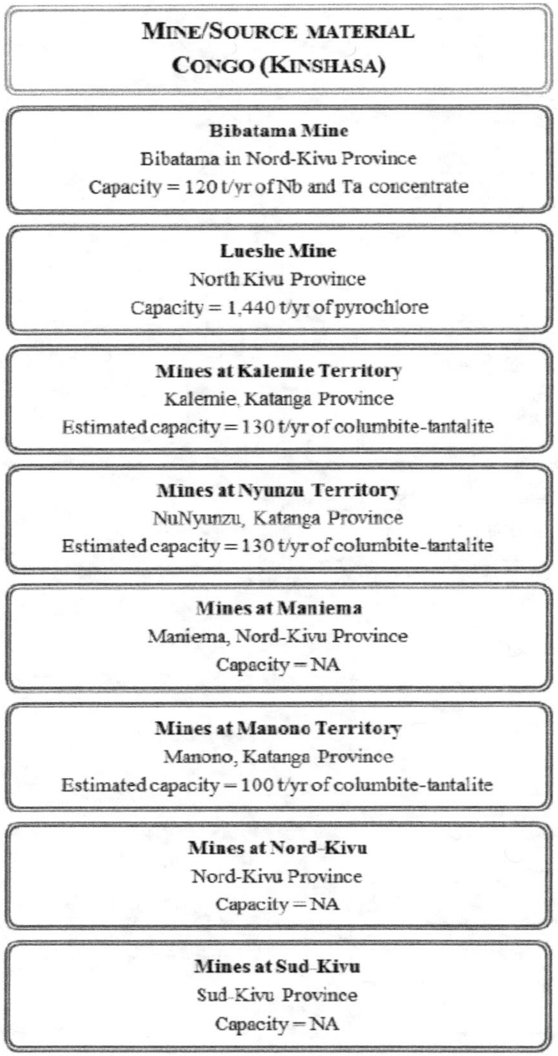

MINE/SOURCE MATERIAL CONGO (KINSHASA)

Bibatama Mine
Bibatama in Nord-Kivu Province
Capacity = 120 t/yr of Nb and Ta concentrate

Lueshe Mine
North Kivu Province
Capacity = 1,440 t/yr of pyrochlore

Mines at Kalemie Territory
Kalemie, Katanga Province
Estimated capacity = 130 t/yr of columbite-tantalite

Mines at Nyunzu Territory
NuNyunzu, Katanga Province
Estimated capacity = 130 t/yr of columbite-tantalite

Mines at Maniema
Maniema, Nord-Kivu Province
Capacity = NA

Mines at Manono Territory
Manono, Katanga Province
Estimated capacity = 100 t/yr of columbite-tantalite

Mines at Nord-Kivu
Nord-Kivu Province
Capacity = NA

Mines at Sud Kivu
Sud Kivu Province
Capacity = NA

23

Figure 6.—Continued

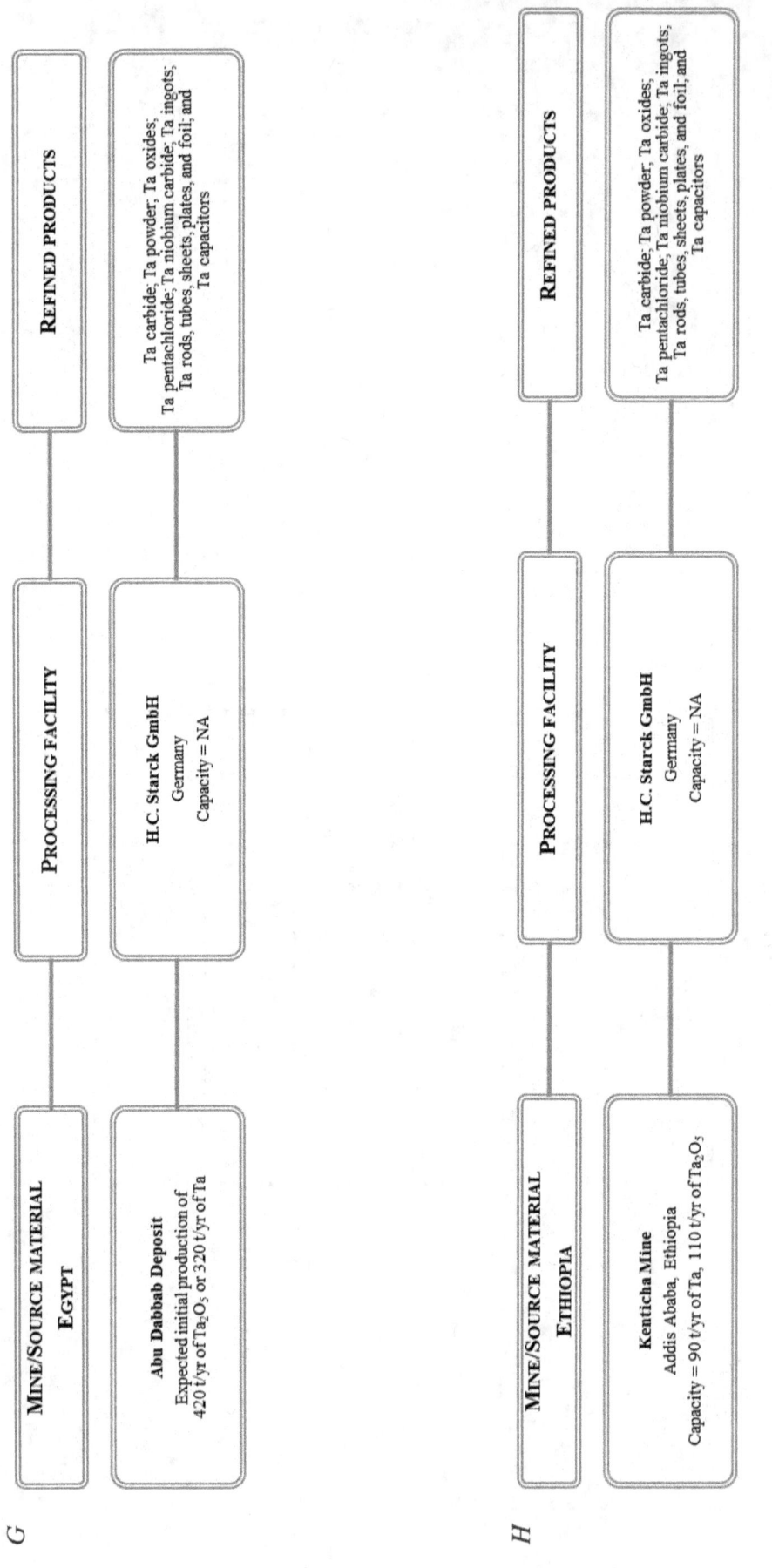

G

MINE/SOURCE MATERIAL EGYPT

Abu Dabbab Deposit
Expected initial production of 420 t/yr of Ta₂O₅ or 320 t/yr of Ta

PROCESSING FACILITY

H.C. Starck GmbH
Germany
Capacity = NA

REFINED PRODUCTS

Ta carbide; Ta powder; Ta oxides;
Ta pentachloride; Ta niobium carbide; Ta ingots;
Ta rods, tubes, sheets, plates, and foil; and
Ta capacitors

H

MINE/SOURCE MATERIAL ETHIOPIA

Kenticha Mine
Addis Ababa, Ethiopia
Capacity = 90 t/yr of Ta, 110 t/yr of Ta₂O₅

PROCESSING FACILITY

H.C. Starck GmbH
Germany
Capacity = NA

REFINED PRODUCTS

Ta carbide; Ta powder; Ta oxides;
Ta pentachloride; Ta niobium carbide; Ta ingots;
Ta rods, tubes, sheets, plates, and foil; and
Ta capacitors

Figure 6.—Continued

24

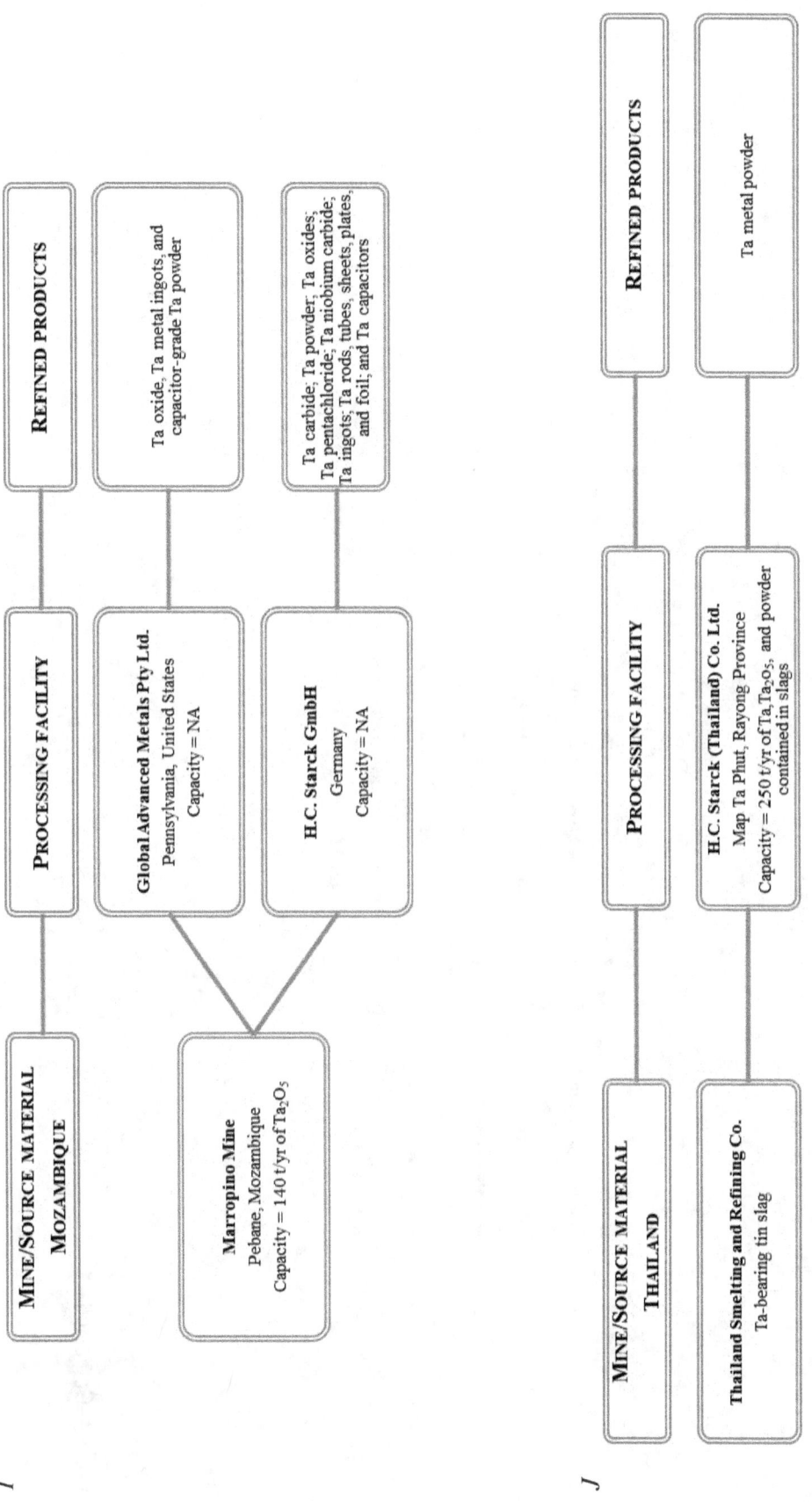

I

MINE/SOURCE MATERIAL MOZAMBIQUE	PROCESSING FACILITY	REFINED PRODUCTS
Marropino Mine Pebane, Mozambique Capacity = 140 t/yr of Ta₂O₅	**Global Advanced Metals Pty Ltd.** Pennsylvania, United States Capacity = NA	Ta oxide, Ta metal ingots, and capacitor-grade Ta powder
	H.C. Starck GmbH Germany Capacity = NA	Ta carbide; Ta powder; Ta oxides; Ta pentachloride; Ta niobium carbide; Ta ingots; Ta rods, tubes, sheets, plates, and foil; and Ta capacitors

J

MINE/SOURCE MATERIAL THAILAND	PROCESSING FACILITY	REFINED PRODUCTS
Thailand Smelting and Refining Co. Ta-bearing tin slag	**H.C. Starck (Thailand) Co. Ltd.** Map Ta Phut, Rayong Province Capacity = 250 t/yr of Ta, Ta₂O₅, and powder contained in slags	Ta metal powder

Figure 6.—Continued

25

K

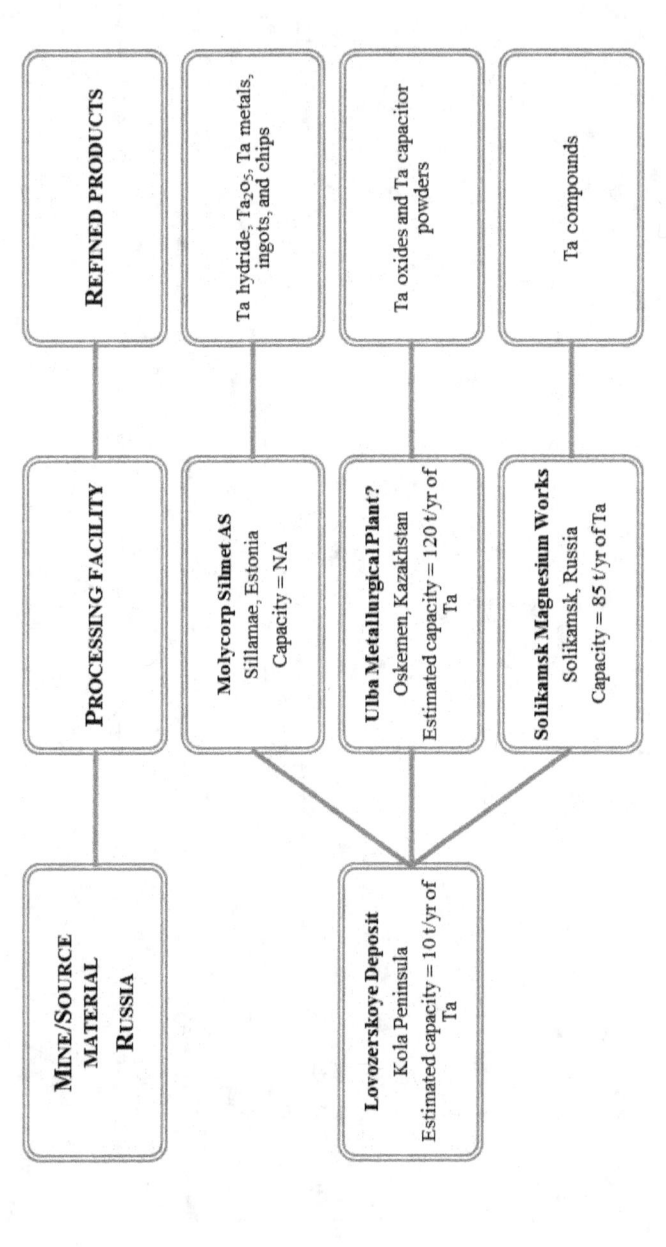

MINE/SOURCE MATERIAL RUSSIA	PROCESSING FACILITY	REFINED PRODUCTS
	Molycorp Silmet AS Sillamae, Estonia Capacity = NA	Ta hydride, Ta₂O₅, Ta metals, ingots, and chips
Lovozerskoye Deposit Kola Peninsula Estimated capacity = 10 t/yr of Ta	**Ulba Metallurgical Plant?** Oskemen, Kazakhstan Estimated capacity = 120 t/yr of Ta	Ta oxides and Ta capacitor powders
	Solikamsk Magnesium Works Solikamsk, Russia Capacity = 85 t/yr of Ta	Ta compounds

26

Figure 6.—Continued

PROCESSING FACILITY

China?

Germany?

MINE/SOURCE MATERIAL
RWANDA

Artisanal Mines
Various sites
Estimated capacity = 8.5 t/yr of Nb, and Ta, columbite-tantalite ore and concentrate

Gihinga Mine
Terimbere Cell
Estimated capacity = 15 t/yr of Nb, and Ta, columbite-tantalite ore and concentrate

Giseke Mine
Nyarubuye Cell
Estimated capacity = 15 t/yr of Nb, and Ta, columbite-tantalite ore and concentrate

Masoro Mine
Kabageshi Cell
Estimated capacity = 34 t/yr of Nb, and Ta, columbite-tantalite ore and concentrate

Mine at Ngororeno District
Ngororeno District
Estimated capacity = 17 t/yr of Nb, and Ta, columbite-tantalite ore and concentrate

Mizbiri Mine
Ruhembe Cell
Estimated capacity = 22 t/yr of Nb, and Ta, columbite-tantalite ore and concentrate

Ndama Mine
Rwikiniro Cell
Estimated capacity = 11 t/yr of Nb, and Ta, columbite-tantalite ore and concentrate

Rubare Mine
Gishyeshye Cell
Estimated capacity = 30 t/yr of Nb, and Ta, columbite-tantalite ore and concentrate

27

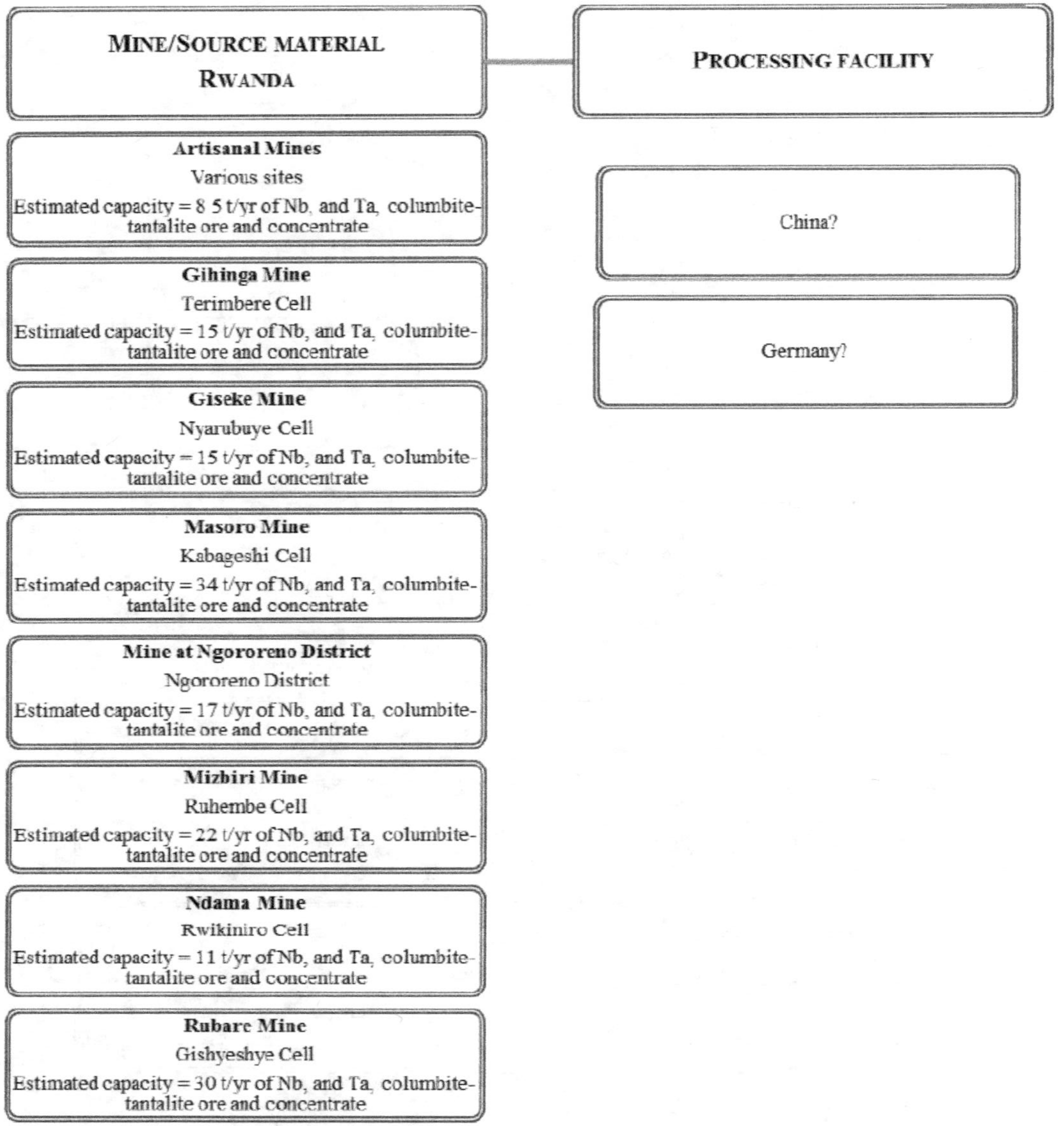

Figure 6.—Continued

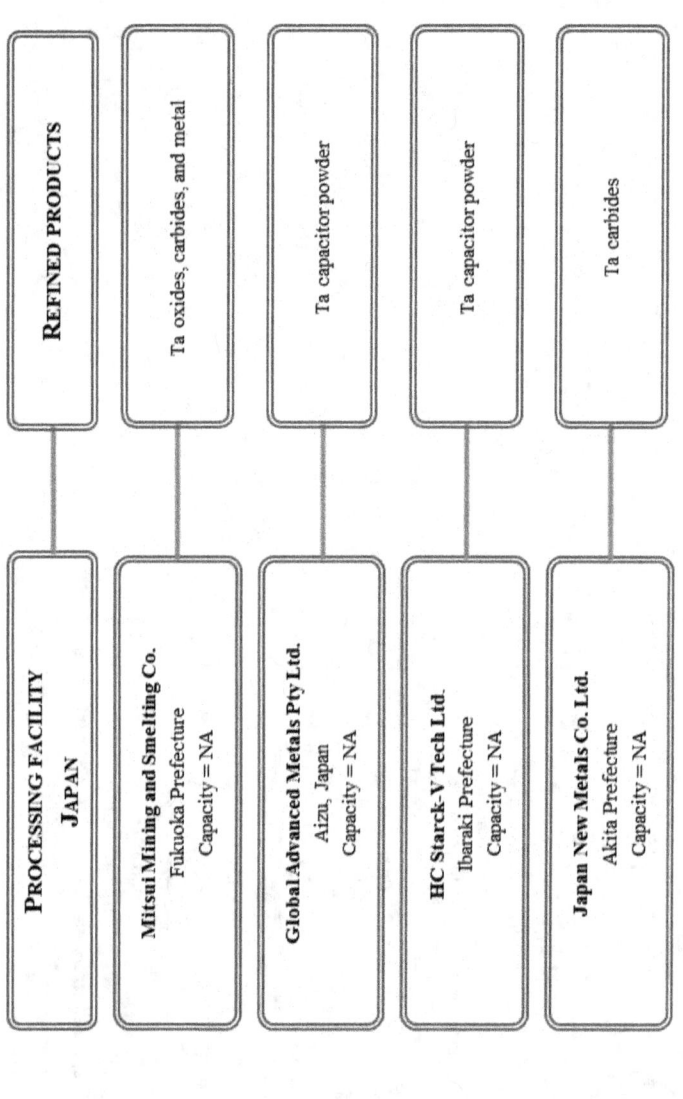

Figure 7. Chart showing tantalum (Ta) refineries in Japan and their products.

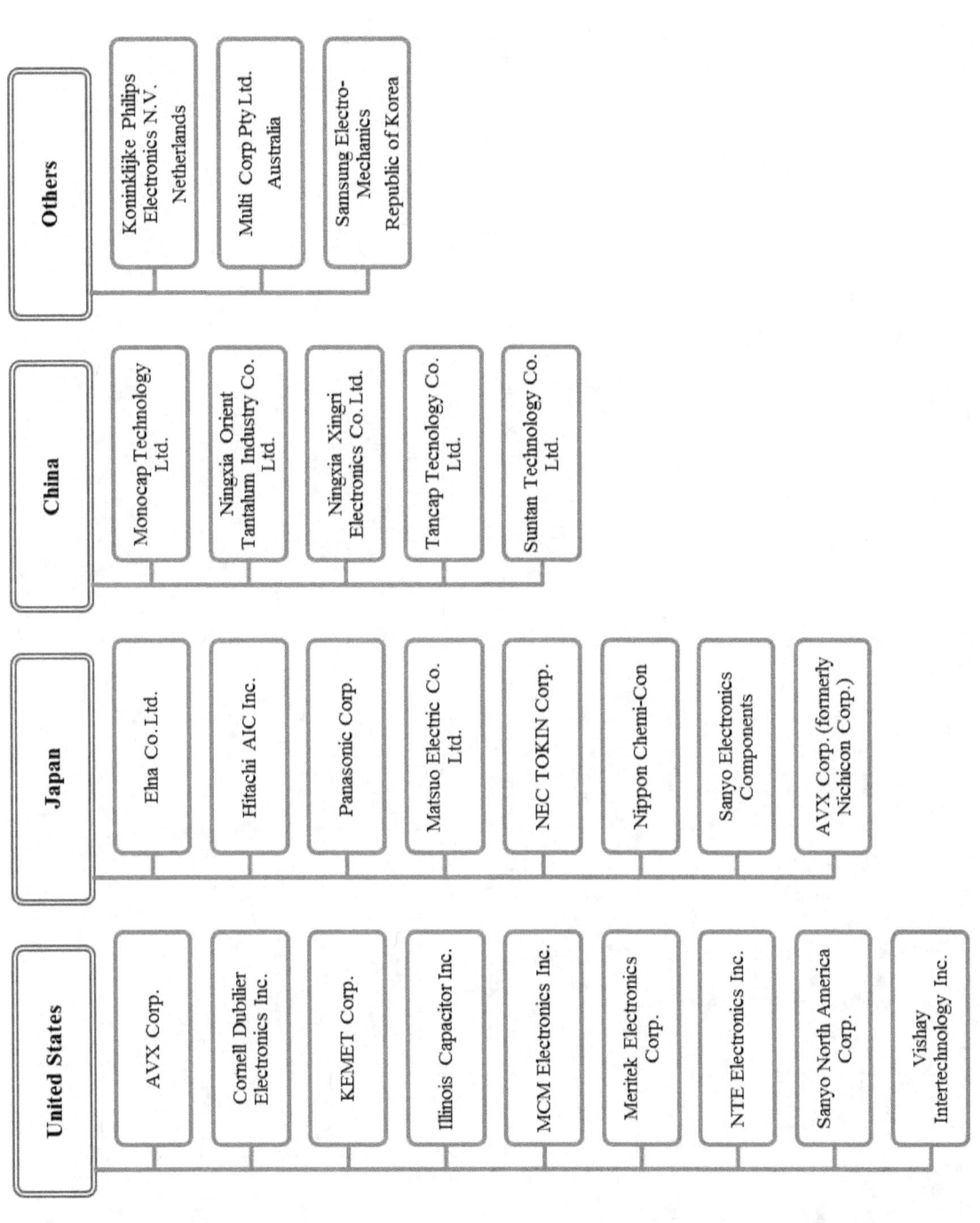

Figure 8. Chart showing selected tantalum capacitor manufacturers.

29

Table 1. Significant tantalum mines.

[Mine locations are shown on the map in figure 3. --, not applicable or no data; A, active; CM, care and maintenance; e, estimated; GL, general location; km, kilometer; M, mine; NA, not available; S, surface/open pit; SL, specific location; SU, surface/open pit and underground; Ta_2O_5, tantalum pentoxide; U, underground. Data are from U.S. Geological Survey Minerals Yearbook 2011, vol. III (http://minerals.usgs.gov/minerals/)]

ID	Year	Specific mineral commodity and (or) product	Country	Location description	Location name	Facility type	Mining method	Ownership	Annual capacity (metric tons)	Status	Latitude (decimal degrees)	Longitude (decimal degrees)	Locational accuracy
1	2011	Tantalum, tantalite, Ta_2O_5	Australia	60 km southeast of Kambalda, Western Australia	Bald Hill tantalite mine	M	SU	Altura Mining Ltd., 100%	100 Ta_2O_5	CM	-31.672	121.894	SL
2	2011	Tantalum, tantalite, Ta_2O_5	Australia	250 km from Perth	Greenbushes open pit/underground tantalite-spodumene mine	M	SU	Global Advanced Metals Pty Ltd., 80% and Traxys Tantalum LP (Traxys Group), 20%	550 Ta_2O_5	A	-33.857	116.051	SL
3	2012	Tantalum, tantalite, Ta_2O_5	Australia	2 km north of Ravensthorpe	Mt. Cattlin Mine	M	S	Galaxy Resources Ltd.	25 Ta_2O_5	A	-33.582	120.048	GL
4	2011	Tantalum, tantalite, Ta_2O_5	Australia	100 km southeast of Port Hedland	Wodgina open pit tantalite mine	M	SU	Global Advanced Metals Pty Ltd., 80%, and Traxys Tantalum LP (Traxys Group), 20%	250 Ta_2O_5	CM	-21.184	118.671	SL
5	2011	Tantalum, concentrate	Brazil	Fluminense Mine, Minas Gerais State	Fluminense Mine (Volta Grande Mine)	M	S	Companhia Industrial Fluminense (AMG Advanced Metallurgical Group N.V.)	25 concentrate	A	-21.084	-44.583	SL
6	2011	Tantalum, concentrate	Brazil	Pitinga Mine, Amazonas State	The Pitinga Mine	M	S	Mineração Taboca S.A. (private, 100%)	180 concentrate	A	-0.784	-60.079	SL
7	2012	Niobium (columbium) and tantalum, columbite-tantalite, ore and concentrate	Burundi	Kabarore, Kayanza Province	Mine at Kabarore	M	--	Comptoir Minier des Exploitations du Burundi S.A. (COMEBU)	6^e	A	-2.824	29.581	GL

Table 1. Significant tantalum mines.—Continued

[Mine locations are shown on the map in figure 3. --, not applicable or no data; A, active; CM, care and maintenance; e, estimated; GL, general location; km, kilometer; M, mine; NA, not available; S, surface/open pit; SL, specific location; SU, surface/open pit and underground; Ta$_2$O$_5$, tantalum pentoxide; U, underground. Data are from U.S. Geological Survey Minerals Yearbook 2011, vol. III (http://minerals.usgs.gov/minerals/)]

ID	Year	Specific mineral commodity and (or) product	Country	Location description	Location name	Facility type	Mining method	Ownership	Annual capacity (metric tons)	Status	Latitude (decimal degrees)	Longitude (decimal degrees)	Locational accuracy
8	2012	Niobium (columbium) and tantalum, columbite-tantalite, ore and concentrate	Burundi	Kayanza Province	Mines at Kayanza Province	M	--	Artisanal miners	160[e,1]	A	-3.010	29.656	GL
9	2012	Niobium (columbium) and tantalum, columbite-tantalite, ore and concentrate	Burundi	Kirundo Province	Mines at Kirundo Province	M	--	Artisanal miners	160[e,1]	A	-2.504	30.223	GL
10	2012	Niobium (columbium) and tantalum, columbite-tantalite, ore and concentrate	Burundi	Ngozi Province	Mines at Ngozi Province	M	--	Artisanal miners	160[e,1]	A	-2.918	29.837	GL
11	2011	Tantalum, tantalite, Ta$_2$O$_5$	Canada	Bernic Lake, Manitoba	Tanco Mine	M	S	Cabot Corp., 100%	80 Ta$_2$O$_5$	CM	50.433	-95.450	SL
12	2012	Tantalum	China	Nanping, Fujian Province	Xikeng Mine	M	U	--	NA	A	26.600	118.042	GL
13	2012	Tantalum	China	Yichun, Jiangxi Province	Yichun Tantalum & Niobium Mine	M	S	China Minmetals Corp., Jiangxi Rare Earth Metal and Rare Metals Tungsten Group Co. Ltd.	NA	A	27.649	114.518	GL

31

Table 1. Significant tantalum mines.—Continued

[Mine locations are shown on the map in figure 3. --, not applicable or no data; A, active; CM, care and maintenance; e, estimated; GL, general location; km, kilometer; M, mine; NA, not available; S, surface/open pit; SL, specific location; SU, surface/open pit and underground; Ta₂O₅, tantalum pentoxide; U, underground. Data are from U.S. Geological Survey Minerals Yearbook 2011, vol. III (http://minerals.usgs.gov/minerals/)]

ID	Year	Specific mineral commodity and (or) product	Country	Location description	Location name	Facility type	Mining method	Ownership	Annual capacity (metric tons)	Status	Latitude (decimal degrees)	Longitude (decimal degrees)	Locational accuracy
14	2010	Niobium (columbium) and tantalum	Congo (Kinshasa)	Bibatama in Nord-Kivu Province	Bibatama Mine	M	--	Mwangachuchu Hizi International	120 concentrate	A	-1.579	28.891	GL
15	2011	Niobium (columbium) and tantalum	Congo (Kinshasa)	Lueshe Mine	Fluminense Mine (Volta Grande Mine)	M	--	Société Minière du Kivu (Simikivu) [GfE Metalle und Materialien GmbH, 70%]	1,440 pyrochlore	S	-0.987	29.141	SL
16	2011	Niobium (columbium) and tantalum	Congo (Kinshasa)	Kalemie, Katanga Province	Mines at Kalemie Territory	M	--	Artisanal miners and small-scale miners	130e columbite-tantalite[2]	A	-5.935	29.180	GL
17	2011	Niobium (columbium) and tantalum	Congo (Kinshasa)	Nyunzu, Katanga Province	Mine at Kabarore	M	--	Artisanal miners and small-scale miners	130e columbite-tantalite[2]	A	-5.943	28.014	GL
18	2011	Niobium (columbium) and tantalum	Congo (Kinshasa)	Maniema, Nord-Kivu Province	Mines at Maniema	M	--	Artisanal miners and small-scale miners	--	A	-3.073	26.041	GL
19	2011	Niobium (columbium) and tantalum	Congo (Kinshasa)	Manono, Katanga Province	Mines at Manono Territory	M	--	Artisanal miners and small-scale miners	100e columbite-tantalite	A	-7.309	27.464	GL
20	2011	Niobium (columbium) and tantalum	Congo (Kinshasa)	Nord-Kivu Province	Mines at Nord-Kivu	M	--	Artisanal miners and small-scale miners	NA	A	-07.92	29.046	GL
21	2011	Niobium (columbium) and tantalum	Congo (Kinshasa)	Sud-Kivu Province	Mines at Sud-Kivu	M	--	Artisanal miners and small-scale miners	NA	A	-3.085	28.354	GL
22	2012	Tantalum, ore	Ethiopia	550 km south of Addis Ababa	Kenticha Mine	M	--	Elenito Mineral Development Share Co.	90 tantalum (current)	A (Expansion proposed by 2017)	5.454	39.017	SL

32

Table 1. Significant tantalum mines.—Continued

[Mine locations are shown on the map in figure 3. --, not applicable or no data; A, active; CM, care and maintenance; e, estimated; GL, general location; km, kilometer; M, mine; NA, not available; S, surface/open pit; SL, specific location; SU, surface/open pit and underground; Ta_2O_5, tantalum pentoxide; U, underground. Data are from U.S. Geological Survey Minerals Yearbook 2011, vol. III (http://minerals.usgs.gov/minerals/)]

ID	Year	Specific mineral commodity and (or) product	Country	Location description	Location name	Facility type	Mining method	Ownership	Annual capacity (metric tons)	Status	Latitude (decimal degrees)	Longitude (decimal degrees)	Locational accuracy
23	2011	Niobium (columbium) and tantalum, columbite-tantalite, ore and concentrate	Mozambique	350 km northeast of Quelimane, Zambezia Province	Marropino Mine	M	S	Noventa Ltd. (Highland African Mining Co. Ltd.)	140 Ta_2O_5	A	-16.515	37.907	SL
24	2010	Tantalum, ore	Russia	Zabaykalskiy mining and beneficiation complex	Etykinskoye deposit	M	--	--	10^{e,3}	A	47.560	134.720	GL
25	2010	Tantalum, ore	Russia	Lovozerskoye deposit [Kola Peninsula]	Lovozerskoye deposit [Kola Peninsula]	M	--	--	10^{e,3}	A	67.333	37.000	GL
26	2012	Niobium (columbium) and tantalum, columbite-tantalite, ore and concentrate	Rwanda	Various Sites	Artisanal Mines	M	--	Artisanal miners	85^e	A	-1.940	29.874	GL
27	2012	Niobium (columbium) and tantalum, columbite-tantalite, ore and concentrate	Rwanda	Terimbere Cell	Gihinga Mine	M	--	KODUBU	15^e	A	-1.936	29.500	GL

33

Table 1. Significant tantalum mines.—Continued

[Mine locations are shown on the map in figure 3. --, not applicable or no data; A, active; CM, care and maintenance; e, estimated; GL, general location; km, kilometer; M, mine; NA, not available; S, surface/open pit; SL, specific location; SU, surface/open pit and underground; Ta$_2$O$_5$, tantalum pentoxide; U, underground. Data are from U.S. Geological Survey Minerals Yearbook 2011, vol. III (http://minerals.usgs.gov/minerals/)]

ID	Year	Specific mineral commodity and (or) product	Country	Location description	Location name	Facility type	Mining method	Ownership	Annual capacity (metric tons)	Status	Latitude (decimal degrees)	Longitude (decimal degrees)	Locational accuracy
28	2012	Niobium (columbium) and tantalum, columbite-tantalite, ore and concentrate	Rwanda	Nyarubuye Cell	Giseke Mine	M	--	KUAKA	15^e	A	-2.552	29.829	GL
29	2012	Niobium (columbium) and tantalum, columbite-tantalite, ore and concentrate	Rwanda	Kabageshi Cell	Masoro Mine	M	--	Ets Munsad Minerals	34^e	A	-1.833	30.049	GL
30	2012	Niobium (columbium) and tantalum, columbite-tantalite, ore and concentrate	Rwanda	Ngororeno District	Mine at Ngororeno District	M	--	Gatumba Mining Concessions Ltd. (GMC) (Kivu Gatumba 36 Resources Ltd., 51%, and Government, 49%)	17^e	A	-1.651	29.871	GL
31	2012	Niobium (columbium) and tantalum, columbite-tantalite, ore and concentrate	Rwanda	Ruhembe Cell	Mizbiri Mine	M	--	EPROCOMI	22^e	A	-1.651	29.871	GL

Table 1. Significant tantalum mines.—Continued

[Mine locations are shown on the map in figure 3. --, not applicable or no data; A, active; CM, care and maintenance; e, estimated; GL, general location; km, kilometer; M, mine; NA, not available; S, surface/open pit; SL, specific location; SU, surface/open pit and underground; Ta$_2$O$_5$, tantalum pentoxide; U, underground. Data are from U.S. Geological Survey Minerals Yearbook 2011, vol. III (http://minerals.usgs.gov/minerals/)]

ID	Year	Specific mineral commodity and (or) product	Country	Location description	Location name	Facility type	Mining method	Ownership	Annual capacity (metric tons)	Status	Latitude (decimal degrees)	Longitude (decimal degrees)	Locational accuracy
32	2012	Niobium (columbium) and tantalum, columbite-tantalite, ore and concentrate	Rwanda	Rwikiniro Cell	Ndama Mine	M	--	Vision Mining Co.	11[e]	A	-1.387	30.473	GL
33	2012	Niobium (columbium) and tantalum, columbite-tantalite, ore and concentrate	Rwanda	Gishyeshye Cell	Rubare Mine	M	--	Ets Kalinda	30[e]	A	-1.600	29.463	GL

[1]Combined capacity of facilities corresponding to ID numbers 8 through 10 in this table

[2]Combined capacity of facilities corresponding to ID numbers 16 and 17 in this table

[3]Combined capacity of facilities corresponding to ID numbers 24 and 25 in this table

Table 2. Prospective tantalum deposits and producers in the world.

[Producer locations are shown on the map in figure 4. --, not applicable or no data; A, active; CM, care and maintenance; D, deposit; e, estimated; GL, general location; km, kilometer; M, mine; NA, not available; P_2O_5, phosphorus pentoxide; REO, rare-earth oxide; S, surface/open pit; SL, specific location; SU, surface/open pit and underground; Ta_2O_5, tantalum pentoxide; U, underground; UD, under development. Data are from U.S. Geological Survey Minerals Yearbook 2011, vol. III (http://minerals.usgs.gov/minerals/)]

ID	Specific mineral commodity and (or) product	Country	Location description	Location name	Facility type	Mining method	Ownership	Tonnage (million metric tons)	Grade (parts per million)	Annual capacity (metric tons)	Status	Latitude (decimal degrees)	Longitude (decimal degrees)	Locational accuracy
1	Tantalum	Australia	35 km south of Laverton, Western Australia	Mount Weld	D	S	Lynas Corp. Ltd.	--	--	--	UD	-28.897	122.384	SL
2	Tantalum	Australia	Dubbo, New South Wales	Dubbo Zirconia Project	D	S	Australian Zirconia Ltd., 100% (Alkane Resources Ltd.)	73.2	0.03 Ta_2O_5	600 Ta_2O_5	A	-32.418	148.713	SL
3	Tantalum	Australia	135 km northwest of Alice Springs	Nolans Rare Earths Project	D	S	Arafura Resources Ltd., 100%	47	2.6% REO, 11% P_2O_5	200^e Ta_2O_5	A	-23.617	133.857	SL
4	Tantalum	Canada	100 km southeast of Yellowknife	Nechalacho Rare-Earth Element Deposit	D	U	Avalon Rare Metals Inc., 100%	14.5 (probable reserves)	400 Ta_2O_5	--	UD	62.096	-112.489	SL
5	Tantalum	Canada	10 km north of Blue River	Blue River Tantalum-Niobium Project, Upper Fir Deposit	D	U	Commerce Resource Corp., 100%	36.35 (indicated)/ 6.40 Mt (inferred)	195 Ta_2O_5 / 199 Ta_2O_5	275^e Ta_2O_5	UD	52.232	-119.169	SL
6	Tantalum	Canada	Crevier Township, Lac Saint-Jean Region	Crevier Deposit	D	SU	MDN Inc., 72.5%, and IAMGOLD, 27.5%	25.4 (measured and indicated)/ 15.4 (inferred)	234 Ta_2O_5 /252 Ta_2O_5	100^e Ta_2O_5	UD	49.500	-72.816	SL
7	Tantalum	China	Dajishan, Jiangxi Province	Dajishan Deposit	D	--	Lynas Corp. Ltd.	--	--	--	U	24.583	114.381	GL

36

Table 2. Prospective tantalum deposits and producers in the world.—Continued

[Producer locations are shown on the map in figure 4. --, not applicable or no data; A, active; CM, care and maintenance; D, deposit; e, estimated; GL, general location; km, kilometer; M, mine; NA, not available; P$_2$O$_5$, phosphorus pentoxide; REO, rare-earth oxide; S, surface/open pit; SL, specific location; SU, surface/open pit and underground; Ta$_2$O$_5$, tantalum pentoxide; U, underground; UD, under development. Data are from U.S. Geological Survey Minerals Yearbook 2011, vol. III (http://minerals.usgs.gov/minerals/)]

ID	Specific mineral commodity and (or) product	Country	Location description	Location name	Facility type	Mining method	Ownership	Tonnage (million metric tons)	Grade (parts per million)	Annual capacity (metric tons)	Status	Latitude (decimal degrees)	Longitude (decimal degrees)	Locational accuracy
8	Tantalum	China	Xianghualing, Hunan Province	Xianghualing Deposit	D	--	--	--	--	--	U	25.433	112.533	GL
9	Tantalum	China	Boluo, Guangdong Province	Boluo Deposit	D	--	--	--	--	--	U	23.132	113.267	GL
10	Tantalum	China	Limu, Guangxi Province	Limu Deposit	D	--	--	--	--	--	U	24.850	110.800	GL
11	Tantalum	China	Xiangdong, Hunan Province	Xiangdong Deposit	D	--	--	--	--	--	U	26.492	112.911	GL
12	Tantalum	Egypt	16 km inland from the western shore of the Red Sea	Abu Dabbab and Nuweibi project	M	S	Tantalum Egypt J.S.C. (Egyptian Company for Mineral Resources 50%, and Tantalum International Pty Ltd., 50% (Gippsland Ltd.)	44.5	250 Ta$_2$O$_5$	420 Ta$_2$O$_5$	UD	49.500	-72.816	SL
13	Tantalum	Malawi	150 km from Malawi City, Lilongwe, Mzimba District	Kanyika Niobium Project	D	S	Globe Metals & Mining	60	--	--	UD	-12.813	33.460	SL
14	Tantalum	Mozambique	Zambezia Province	Morrua Mine	D	S	Noventa Ltd. (Highland Africa Mining Co. Ltd.)	4.6 (indicated)/ 3 1 (inferred)	--	--	CM	-16.270	37.866	SL

37

Table 2. Prospective tantalum deposits and producers in the world.—Continued

[Producer locations are shown on the map in figure 4. --, not applicable or no data; A, active; CM, care and maintenance; D, deposit; e, estimated; GL, general location; km, kilometer; M, mine; NA, not available; P_2O_5, phosphorus pentoxide; REO, rare-earth oxide; S, surface/open pit; SL, specific location; SU, surface/open pit and underground; Ta_2O_5, tantalum pentoxide; U, underground; UD, under development. Data are from U.S. Geological Survey Minerals Yearbook 2011, vol. III (http://minerals.usgs.gov/minerals/)]

ID	Specific mineral commodity and (or) product	Country	Location description	Location name	Facility type	Mining method	Ownership	Tonnage (million metric tons)	Grade (parts per million)	Annual capacity (metric tons)	Status	Latitude (decimal degrees)	Longitude (decimal degrees)	Locational accuracy
15	Tantalum	Mozambique	Zambezia Province	Mutala Mine	D	S	Noventa Ltd. (Highland Africa Mining Co. Ltd.)	--	--	--	CM	-15.930	37.912	SL
16	Tantalum	Saudi Arabia	Tabuk	Ghurayyah Tantalum-Niobium REE Project	D	--	Tertiary Minerals plc, 50%, AH Algosaibi Bros Co., 25%, and Al Nahla Trading & Contracting Co., 25%	400 (inferred)	245 Ta_2O_5	275e Ta_2O_5	S	28.375	36.527	GL

Table 3. Significant tantalum plants (fabricators and refineries).

[Locations of fabricators and refineries are shown on the map in figure 5. --, not applicable or no data; ?, uncertain; A, active; e, estimated; F, fabricator; GL, general location; NA, not available; P, plant; R, refinery; SL, specific location. Data are from U.S. Geological Survey Minerals Yearbook 2011, vol. III (http://minerals.usgs.gov/minerals/)]

ID	Year	Specific mineral commodity and (or) product	Country	Location description	Location name	Facility type	Ownership	Annual capacity (metric tons)	Status	Latitude (decimal degrees)	Longitude (decimal degrees)	Locational accuracy
1	2012	Tantalum	Austria	Althofen, Carinthia	Treibacher Industrie AG	P (F)	Treibacher Industrie AG	--	A	46.867	14.460	SL
2	2012	Tantalum	Austria	Liezen	PLANSEE Liezen	P (F)	Plansee SE, 100%	--	A	47.561	14.247	SL
3	2012	Tantalum	Brazil	Sao Joao del Rei, Minas Gerais	Companhia Industrial Fluminense	P (R)	Companhia Industrial Fluminense (AMG Advanced Metallurgical Group N.V.)	--	A	-21.084	-44.583	SL
4	2012	Tantalum	China	Ye Jin Road, Shizuishan City, Ningxia Province	Ningxia Non-Ferrous Metal Smelter	P (R)	Ningxia Non-ferrous Metal Smelter	300^e tantalum powder, 120^e tantalum wire, 30^e tantalum oxide, 25^e tantalum metal, 6^e tantalum tube	A	38.994	106.375	GL
5	2012	Tantalum	China	Shishi Industrial Zone, Yifeng, Jiangxi Province	King-Tan Tantalum Industry Ltd.	P (R)	King-Tan Tantalum Industry Ltd.	350^e tantalum powder, 120^e t wire, 30^e t oxide, 25^e tantalum metal, 30^e carbide	A	28.256	114.777	GL
6	2012	Tantalum	China	Conghua, Guangdong Province	Conghua Tantalum and Niobium Smelter	P (R?)	Conghua Tantalum & Niobium Smelter	50^e tantalum powder, 70^e tantalum oxide	A	23.548	113.587	GL
7	2012	Tantalum	China	Jiangxi Province	Jiujiang Tanbre's Smelter	P (R?)	Jiangxi Tungsten Group Limited Corp.	50^e tantalum metal, 100^e tantalum oxide	A	29.705	116.002	GL

Table 3. Significant tantalum plants (fabricators and refineries).—Continued

[Locations of fabricators and refineries are shown on the map in figure 5. --, not applicable or no data; ?, uncertain; A, active; e, estimated; F, fabricator; GL, general location; NA, not available; P, plant; R, refinery; SL, specific location. Data are from U.S. Geological Survey Minerals Yearbook 2011, vol. III (http://minerals.usgs.gov/minerals/)]

ID	Year	Specific mineral commodity and (or) product	Country	Location description	Location name	Facility type	Ownership	Annual capacity (metric tons)	Status	Latitude (decimal degrees)	Longitude (decimal degrees)	Locational accuracy
8	2012	Tantalum	Estonia	Sillamae	Molycorp Silmet AS	P (R)	Molycorp Inc., 90%	--	A	59.401	27.746	GL
9	2012	Tantalum	Germany	Im Schleek, Goslar	Goslar Plant	P (R)	H.C. Starck GmbH	--	A	51.909	10.474	SL
10	2012	Tantalum	Germany	Ferroweg, Laufenburg	Rhina Plant	P (R)	H.C. Starck GmbH	--	A	47.556	8.039	SL
11	2012	Tantalum	Germany	Sackinger Strasse, Laufenburg	ENAG Plant	P (R)	H.C. Starck GmbH	--	A	47.559	8.048	SL
12	2012	Tantalum	Germany	Hanau	Heraeus Material Technology GmbH & Co. KG	P (F?)	Heraeus Holding GmbH	--	A	50.131	8.925	SL
13	2012	Tantalum and niobium	Japan	Akita, Akita Prefecture	Akita	P (R?)	Japan New Metals Co. Ltd.	95^e concentrate	A	39.760	140.065	GL
14	2012	Tantalum and niobium	Japan	Aizuwakamatsu-shi, Fukushima prefecture	Aizu Refinery Plant	P (R?)	Global Advanced Metals Pty Ltd.	--	A	37.460	139.936	GL
15	2012	Tantalum and niobium	Japan	Fukuoka prefecture	Miike Rare Metal	P (R)	Mitsui Mining and Smelting Co. Ltd.	NA	A	33.606	130.419	GL
16	2012	Tantalum and niobium	Japan	Hitachi-Ohmiya, Ibaraki prefecture	H.C. Starck-V Tech Ltd.	P (R)	H.C. Starck GmbH	NA	A	36.506	140.615	GL
17	2012	Tantalum, metal	Kazakhstan	Oskemen (also known as Ust-Kamenogorsk)	Oskemen (also known as Ust-Kamenogorsk)	P (R)	Ulba Metallurgical Plant	NA	A	49.982	82.627	SL
18	2012	Tantalum	Russia	Solikamsk, Perm Krai	Solikamsk Magnesium Works	P (R)	Solikamsk Magnesium Works	85	A	59.634	56.767	GL

Table 3. Significant tantalum plants (fabricators and refineries).—Continued

[Locations of fabricators and refineries are shown on the map in figure 5. --, not applicable or no data; ?, uncertain; A, active; e, estimated; F, fabricator; GL, general location; NA, not available; P, plant; R, refinery; SL, specific location. Data are from U.S. Geological Survey Minerals Yearbook 2011, vol. III (http://minerals.usgs.gov/minerals/)]

ID	Year	Specific mineral commodity and (or) product	Country	Location description	Location name	Facility type	Ownership	Annual capacity (metric tons)	Status	Latitude (decimal degrees)	Longitude (decimal degrees)	Locational accuracy
19	2012	Tantalum, metal powder and oxides	Thailand	Map Ta Phut, Rayong Province	H.C. Starck (Thailand) Company Ltd.	P (R)	H.C. Starck (Thailand) Company Ltd. (H.C. Starck GmbH, 94.98%, and others, 5.02%)	250 contained in slags	A	12.688	101.141	SL
20	2012	Tantalum	United States	Boyertown, Pennsylvania	Boyertown Plant	P (R)	Global Advanced Metals Pty Ltd.	--	A	40.346	-75.612	SL
21	2012	Tantalum	United States	Newton, Massachusetts	H.C. Starck Inc.	P (R)	H.C. Starck Inc.	--	A	42.311	-71.214	SL
22	2012	Tantalum	United States	Carson City, Nevada	KEMET Blue Powder Corp.	P (F)	KEMET Corp.	--	A	39.234	-119.657	SL

41

Table 4. Locations of tantalum capacitor manufacturing facilities for three leading manufacturers.

[Sources: AVX Corp. (2013a), KEMET Corp. (2012b, d), and NEC TOKIN Corp. (2013)]

Manufacturing company	Tantalum capacitor manufacturing location
AVX Corp.	Adogawa, Japan (formerly Nichicon Corp.)
	Bidderford, Maine, USA
	Lanskroun, Czech Republic
	San Salvador, El Salvador
	Tianjin, China (formerly Nichicon Corp.)
KEMET Corp.	Carson City, Nevada, USA
	Cuidad Victoria, Mexico
	Evora, Portugal
	Matamoros, Mexico
	Suzhou, China (2 facilities)
NEC TOKIN Corp.	Sendai City, Miyagi, Japan
	Shiroishi City, Miyagi, Japan
	Nyuzen-machi, Shimoniikawa District, Toyama, Japan
	NEC TOKIN Electronics (Thailand) Co. Ltd.
	NEC TOKIN Electronics (Xiamen) Corp.
	NEC TOKIN Electronics (Philippines) Inc.
	NEC TOKIN Electronics (Vietnam) Co. Ltd.

Table 5. Product name, description, and applications for selected tantalum capacitors produced by AVX Corp.

[Source: AVX Corp. (2013b)]

Tantalum capacitors	Description	Applications
TAZ Series	CWR09-MIL-PRF-55365/4; CWR19 MIL-PRF-55365/11; CWR29 MIL-PRF-55365/11; Extended Range-63V COTS-Plus Rating	• Include medical devices and military/aerospace.
TCP Series	TCP Series Low ESR Tantalum Modules	
TBJ Series	CWR11- MIL-PRF-55365/8 Established Reliability, COTS-Plus & Space Level; COTS-PLUS-DSCC Dwgs 07016 & 95158 Weibull Grade & Space Level	
TBM Multianode	Tantalum Ultra Low ESR COTS-Plus Weibull Grade & Space Level	
TBW Series	Tantalum Fused DSCC Dwg 04053 COTS-Plus Weibull Grade & Space Level	
TBC Series	CWR15 MIL-PRF-55365/12 Established Reliability, COTS-Plus & Space Level; TBC COTS-Plus	
TWA Series	TWA Wet Electrolytic Tantalum Capacitor	
TWM Module	AVX modular packaged 93026 qualified capacitors	
TAJ ESCC Tantalum Capacitors	SMD Solid Tantalum Chip Capacitors	
TAJ CECC Tantalum Capacitors	SMD Solid Tantalum Chip Capacitors	

Table 6. Product name, product description, and applications for selected tantalum (Ta) capacitors produced by KEMET Corp.

[ABS, anti-lock braking system; DC, direct current; DSCC, Defense Supply Center Columbus; ESL, Equivalent Series Inductance; HDD, hard disk drive; kHz, kilohertz; MnO$_2$, manganese oxide; PC, personal computer; SSD, solid-state drive; USB, Universal Serial Bus (USB); V, volt. Source: KEMET Corp. (2013a, b)]

Tantalum capacitors	Description	Applications
Tantalum Surface Mount Capacitors Standard Tantalum	T491 Industrial Grade MnO$_2$ Series	• Include decoupling and filtering in industrial and automotive end applications, such as DC/DC converters, portable electronics, telecommunications, and control units.
Tantalum Surface Mount Capacitors Low Equivalent Series Resistance (ESR)	MnO$_2$ T494 Industrial Grade Low ESR MnO$_2$ Series	
	T495 Surge Robust Low ESR MnO$_2$ Series T510 Multiple Anode Low ESR MnO$_2$ Series	• Include decoupling and filtering in industrial and automotive end applications, such as DC/DC converters, portable electronics, telecommunications, and control units requiring high-ripple-current capability.
	Tantalum Stack MnO$_2$ (TSM) Series	• Include decoupling and filtering in a variety of market segments. The T493 COTS stack devices can be utilized in military and aerospace applications. Other KEMET series can be utilized in filtering and decoupling applications to service various market segments.
	Polymer T520 Series Polymer Tantalum	• Include DC/DC converters, notebook PCs, portable electronics, telecommunications (cell phone and base station), displays, SSD, HDD and USB.
	T521 High Voltage Polymer Tantalum	• Include DC/DC converters, power supply input and higher voltage applications, such as 12V to 28V power input rails in the military/aerospace and industrial markets.
	T525 125°C Rated Polymer Tantalum	• Include automotive, industrial, and military as per DSCC 04051.
	T528 Low ESL/Facedown Terminal Polymer Tantalum T530 High Capacitance/125°C Rated Polymer Tantalum	• Include high-speed server, microprocessor decoupling, and high-ripple-current applications.
	KEMET Organic Capacitor (AO-CAP) A700 Series Polymer Aluminum	• Include DC/DC converters, notebook PCs, telecommunications, displays, and industrial applications.

Table 6. Product name, product description, and applications for selected tantalum (Ta) capacitors produced by KEMET Corp.—Continued

[ABS, anti-lock braking system; DC, direct current; DSCC, Defense Supply Center Columbus; ESL, Equivalent Series Inductance; HDD, hard disk drive; kHz, kilohertz; MnO_2, manganese oxide; PC, personal computer; SSD, solid-state drive; USB, Universal Serial Bus (USB); V, volt. Source: KEMET Corp. (2013a, b)]

Tantalum capacitors	Description	Applications
Tantalum Surface Mount Capacitors High Temperature	T498 150°C Rated MnO_2 Series T499 175°C Rated MnO_2 Series	• Include decoupling and filtering in industrial and automotive end applications, such as DC/DC converters, portable electronics, telecommunications, and control units operating at temperatures up to 175°C.
Tantalum Surface Mount Capacitors MIL-PRF (CWR Series)	T409 Series CWR09 Style MIL-PRF-55365/4 T419 Series CWR19 Style MIL-PRF-55365/11 T429 Series CWR29 Style MIL-PRF-55365/8 T492 CWR11 Style MIL-PRF-55365/8	• Include decoupling and filtering in military and aerospace applications requiring CWR09, CWR19, CW29, and CRWR11 devices (precision-molded devices with compliant terminations and indelible laser marking).
Tantalum Surface Mount Capacitors Fused	T496 Fused MnO_2 Series	• Include decoupling and filtering in computing and telecommunications end applications, such as high-end servers requiring built-in fuse capability.
Tantalum Surface Mount Capacitors High Reliability Commercial-Off-The-Shelf (COTS)	T493 Military/Aerospace COTS MnO_2 Series	• Include decoupling and filtering in military and aerospace applications
	T497 High Grade COTS MnO_2 Series	• Include decoupling and filtering in military, medical, and aerospace applications.
	T540 Polymer COTS Series T541 Polymer COTS Series	• Include decoupling and filtering in military and aerospace applications that require low ESR or a benign failure mode.
Tantalum Surface Mount Capacitors Automotive Grade	T491 Industrial Grade MnO_2 Series T494 Industrial Grade Low ESR MnO_2 Series	• Include decoupling and filtering in industrial and automotive end applications, such as DC/DC converters, portable electronics, telecommunications, and control units.
	T489 Low Leakage MnO_2 Series	• Include decoupling and filtering in industrial and automotive high-end applications.

Table 6. Product name, product description, and applications for selected tantalum (Ta) capacitors produced by KEMET Corp.—Continued

[ABS, anti-lock braking system; DC, direct current; DSCC, Defense Supply Center Columbus; ESL, Equivalent Series Inductance; HDD, hard disk drive; kHz, kilohertz; MnO_2, manganese oxide; PC, personal computer; SSD, solid-state drive; USB, Universal Serial Bus (USB); V, volt. Source: KEMET Corp. (2013a, b)]

Tantalum capacitors	Description	Applications
Tantalum Surface Mount Capacitors Automotive Grade—Continued	T495 Surge Robust Low ESR MnO_2 MnO_2 Series	• Include decoupling and filtering in industrial and automotive end applications, such as DC/DC converters, portable electronics, telecommunications, and control units requiring high-ripple-current capability.
	T498 150°C Rated MnO_2 Series T499 175°C Rated MnO_2 Series	• Include decoupling and filtering in industrial and automotive end applications, such as DC/DC converters, portable electronics, telecommunications, and control units operating at temperatures up 175°C,.
	T510 Multiple Anode Low ESR MnO_2 Series	• Include decoupling and filtering in industrial and automotive end applications, such as DC/DC converters, portable electronics, telecommunications, and control units requiring high-ripple-current capability.
	T525 125°C Rated Polymer Tantalum	• Include automotive, industrial, and military applications as per DSCC 04051.
Tantalum Surface Mount Capacitors Space Grade	T493 Series COTS Space Grade	• Include decoupling and filtering in military and aerospace applications.
	T496 Series Fail-Safe Fused Space Grade	• Include decoupling and filtering in computing and telecommunications end applications, such as high-end servers requiring built-in fuse capability.
	T497 Series High Grade COTS Space Grade	• Include decoupling and filtering in military, medical, and aerospace applications.
	T510 Series Multiple Anode Low ESR Space Grade	• Include decoupling and filtering in industrial and automotive end applications, such as DC/DC converters, portable electronics, telecommunications, and control units requiring-high ripple-current capability.

Table 6. Product name, product description, and applications for selected tantalum (Ta) capacitors produced by KEMET Corp.—Continued

[ABS, anti-lock braking system; DC, direct current; DSCC, Defense Supply Center Columbus; ESL, Equivalent Series Inductance; HDD, hard disk drive; kHz, kilohertz; MnO_2, manganese oxide; PC, personal computer; SSD, solid-state drive; USB, Universal Serial Bus (USB); V, volt. Source: KEMET Corp. (2013a, b)]

Tantalum capacitors	Description	Applications
T409 Series	T409 Series CWR09 Style MIL-PRF-55365/4	• Include decoupling and filtering in military and aerospace applications requiring CWR09 devices.
T419 Series	T419 Series CWR19 Style MIL-PRF-55365/11	• Include decoupling and filtering in military and aerospace applications requiring CWR19 devices.
T429 Series	T429 Series CWR29 Style MIL-PRF-55365/8	• Include decoupling and filtering in military and aerospace applications requiring CWR29 devices.
T489 Series	T489 Low DC Leakage MnO_2 Series	• Include decoupling and filtering in industrial and automotive high-end applications.
T491 Series	T491 Industrial Grade MnO_2 Series	• Not available.
T492 Series	T492 CWR11 Style MIL-PRF-55365/8	• Include decoupling and filtering in military and aerospace applications requiring CWR11 devices.
T493 Series (COTS)	T493 Series - Approved to DSCC Drawing 07016-Military/Aerospace COTS MnO_2	• Include decoupling and filtering in military and aerospace applications.
T493 Series Space Grade	T493 Series COTS (CWR11 Style)	• Include decoupling and filtering in military and aerospace applications.
T494 Series	T494 Industrial Grade Low ESR MnO_2 Series	• Include decoupling and filtering in industrial and automotive end applications, such as DC/DC converters, portable electronics, telecommunications, and control units.
T495 Series	T495 Surge Robust Low ESR MnO_2 Series	• Include decoupling and filtering in industrial and automotive end applications, such as DC/DC converters, portable electronics, telecommunications, and control units requiring high–ripple-current capability.
T496 Series	T496 Fused MnO_2 Series	• Include decoupling and filtering in computing and telecommunications end applications, such as high-end servers requiring built-in fuse capability.
T496 Series - Approved to DSCC Drawing 04053- Fail-Safe Fused Tantalum Chip	T496 Series - Approved to DSCC Drawing 04053- Fail-Safe Fused Tantalum Chip	• Not available.

Table 6. Product name, product description, and applications for selected tantalum (Ta) capacitors produced by KEMET Corp.—Continued

[ABS, anti-lock braking system; DC, direct current; DSCC, Defense Supply Center Columbus; ESL, Equivalent Series Inductance; HDD, hard disk drive; kHz, kilohertz; MnO_2, manganese oxide; PC, personal computer; SSD, solid-state drive; USB, Universal Serial Bus (USB); V, volt. Source: KEMET Corp. (2013a, b)]

Tantalum capacitors	Description	Applications
T496 Series Space Grade	T496 Series Fail-Safe Fused MnO_2	• Military and aerospace customers in high-reliability space applications.
T497 Series	T497 High Grade COTS MnO_2 Series	• Include decoupling and filtering in military, medical, and aerospace applications.
T497 Series Space Grade	T497 Series High Grade COTS (CWR09/19/29 Style)	
T498 Series	T498 150°C Rated MnO_2 Series	• Include decoupling and filtering in industrial and automotive end applications, such as DC/DC converters, portable electronics, telecommunications, and control units operating at temperatures up to 150°C.
T499 Series	T499 175°C Rated MnO_2 Series	• Include decoupling and filtering in industrial and automotive end applications, such as DC/DC converters, portable electronics, telecommunications, and control units operating at temperatures up to 175°C.
T510 Series	T510 Multiple Anode Low ESR MnO_2 Series	• Include decoupling and filtering in industrial and automotive end applications, such as DC/DC converters, portable electronics, telecommunications, and control units requiring high–ripple-current capability.
T510 Series Space Grade	T510 Series Multiple Anode Low ESR MnO_2	
T513 Series	T513 Multiple Anode Low ESR COTS MnO_2 Series	• Suitable for the industrial, communications, military, and aerospace markets. Typical applications include decoupling and filtering in radar, sonar, power supply, guidance systems, and other high-reliability applications.
TSM Series	TSM Series Tantalum MnO_2 Surface Mount Stack Capacitors	• Include decoupling and filtering in a variety of market segments. The T493 COTS and 540 stack devices can be utilized in military and aerospace applications. Other KEMET series can be utilized in filtering and decoupling applications to service various market segments.
TSP Series	TSP Series Tantalum Stack Polymer Surface Mount Capacitors	

Table 6. Product name, product description, and applications for selected tantalum (Ta) capacitors produced by KEMET Corp.—Continued

[ABS, anti-lock braking system; DC, direct current; DSCC, Defense Supply Center Columbus; ESL, Equivalent Series Inductance; HDD, hard disk drive; kHz, kilohertz; MnO$_2$, manganese oxide; PC, personal computer; SSD, solid-state drive; USB, Universal Serial Bus (USB); V, volt. Source: KEMET Corp. (2013a, b)]

Tantalum capacitors	Description	Applications
T540 Series	T540 Polymer COTS	• Include decoupling and filtering in military and aerospace applications that require low ESR or a benign failure mode.
T541 Series	T541 Polymer COTS Multiple Anode	
T520 Series	T520 Series Polymer Tantalum	• Include DC/DC converters, notebook PCs, portable electronics, telecommunications (cell phone and base station), displays, SSD, HDD and USB.
T521 Series	T521 High Voltage Polymer Tantalum	• Include DC/DC converters, power supply input, and higher voltage applications, such as 12V to 50V power input rails in the military, aerospace, and industrial markets.
T522 Series	T522 Reduced Leakage Polymer Tantalum	• Include battery-dependent applications, such as handheld consumer electronics, global tracking systems, energy harvesting, wireless sensors, and other applications that seek high capacitance, low profile, safety, and low power consumption.
T525 Series	T525 125°C Rated Polymer Tantalum	• Include automotive, industrial, and military applications as per DSCC 04051.
T525 Series - Approved to DSCC Drawing 04051 - High-Temperature Tantalum Chip	T525 Series - Approved to DSCC Drawing 04051 - High-Temperature Tantalum Chip	• Not available.
T528 Series	T528 Low ESL/Facedown Terminal Polymer Tantalum	• Include high-speed server, microprocessor decoupling, and high-ripple-current applications.
T530 Series	T530 High Capacitance/125°C Rated Polymer Tantalum	
T530 Series - Approved to DSCC Drawing 04052 - High-Capacitance/Ultra-Low ESR Tantalum Chip	T530 Series - Approved to DSCC Drawing 04052 - High-Capacitance/Ultra-Low ESR Tantalum Chip	• Not available.

Table 6. Product name, product description, and applications for selected tantalum (Ta) capacitors produced by KEMET Corp.—Continued

[ABS, anti-lock braking system; DC, direct current; DSCC, Defense Supply Center Columbus; ESL, Equivalent Series Inductance; HDD, hard disk drive; kHz, kilohertz; MnO_2, manganese oxide; PC, personal computer; SSD, solid-state drive; USB, Universal Serial Bus (USB); V, volt. Source: KEMET Corp. (2013a, b)]

Tantalum capacitors	Description	Applications
B45 Series - Automotive	B45196L, B45198L	• Automotive electronics (for example, safety applications: airbags, ABS, motor management) • Measuring and control engineering (for example, voltage regulators), and DC/DC converters
B45 Series - High Capacitance	B45196E/H, B45198E/HL	• Telecommunications (for example, cell phones, infrastructure) • Data processing (for example, laptops, mainframes) • Measuring and control engineering (for example, voltage regulators) • Automotive electronics (for example, safety applications—airbags, ABS, motor management) • Medical engineering • DC/DC converters
B45 Series - High Temperature	B45196T, B45198T	• Automotive electronics (for example, safety applications—airbags, ABS, motor management, electronic control unit) • Measuring and control engineering (for example, voltage regulators) • Medical engineering • DC/DC converters • Telecommunications (for example, cell phones, infrastructure) • Data processing (for example, laptops, mainframes)
B45 Series - Low Profile	B450, B45190E/R, B45192E/R, B45194E/R	• Telecommunications (for example, cell phones, infrastructure) • Data processing (for example, laptops, mainframes) • Measuring and control engineering (for example, voltage regulators) • Automotive electronics (for example, navigation systems, electronic control units) • Medical engineering • Switch mode power supplies with very high clock frequencies (300 kHz) • DC/DC converters

Table 6. Product name, product description, and applications for selected tantalum (Ta) capacitors produced by KEMET Corp.—Continued

[ABS, anti-lock braking system; DC, direct current; DSCC, Defense Supply Center Columbus; ESL, Equivalent Series Inductance; HDD, hard disk drive; kHz, kilohertz; MnO_2, manganese oxide; PC, personal computer; SSD, solid-state drive; USB, Universal Serial Bus (USB); V, volt. Source: KEMET Corp. (2013a, b)]

Tantalum capacitors	Description	Applications
B45 Series - Multiple Anode	B45396R	• Telecommunications (for example, cell phones, infrastructure) • Data processing (for example, laptops, mainframes) • Measuring and control engineering (for example, voltage regulators) • Medical engineering • DC/DC converters
B45 Series - Performance	B45196P, B45198P	• Automotive electronics (for example, safety applications—airbags, ABS, motor management) • Measuring and control engineering • Medical engineering • DC/DC converters • Telecommunications (for example, cell phones, infrastructure) • Data processing (for example, laptops, mainframes)
B45 Series - SpeedPower	B450, B451, B45197A, B45198R	• Telecommunications (for example, cell phones, infrastructure) • Data processing (for example, laptops, mainframes) • Measuring and control engineering (for example, voltage regulators) • Automotive electronics (for example, navigation systems, electronic control units) • Medical engineering • DC/DC converters
B76 Series - Conductive Polymer	B760	• Not available.